W9-APX-804

THE GOD WHO ACTS

BT
135
.G634

Edited by Thomas F. Tracy

THE GOD WHO ACTS

Philosophical
and
Theological Explorations

The Pennsylvania State University Press
University Park, Pennsylvania

FEB 1 9 1997

491978

Library of Congress Cataloging-in-Publication Data

The God who acts : philosophical and theological explorations / edited
  by Thomas F. Tracy.
        p.   cm.
    Includes bibliographical references (p. xxx–xxx) and index.
    ISBN 0-271-01039-8 (cloth : alk. paper). — ISBN 0-271-01040-1
    (pbk.)
    1. Providence and government of God—Congresses. 2. Good and
evil—Congresses. 3. Free will and determinism—Congresses.
4. Theodicy—Congresses. 5. Creation—Congresses. 6. Sin
—Congresses. I. Tracy, Thomas F., 1948– .
  BT135.G634   1994
  214'.8—dc20   93-29637
                                                          CIP

Copyright © 1994 The Pennsylvania State University
All rights reserved
Printed in the United States of America

Published by The Pennsylvania State University Press,
University Park, PA 16802-1003

It is the policy of The Pennsylvania State University Press to use acid-free paper for the
first printing of all clothbound books. Publications on uncoated stock satisfy the minimum
requirements of American National Standard for Information Sciences—Permanence of
Paper for Printed Library Materials, ANSI Z39.48–1984.

CONTENTS

ACKNOWLEDGMENTS

Initial drafts of most of the chapters included in this volume were presented at a research conference held at the University of California at Los Angeles. The conference was funded by the university through the College of Letters and Sciences and was sponsored by the Department of Philosophy. The opportunity to organize the conference was made available to me by Robert Adams, whose own writings are a rich source of insightful philosophical reflection on theological topics. The work of assembling and editing these essays stretched over a considerable period of time that included part of the term of a fellowship from the National Endowment for the Humanities. I am grateful to UCLA and to the NEH for their support.

CONTRIBUTORS

Robert Merrihew Adams is chair of the Department of Philosophy at Yale University. He is well known for his work in philosophy of religion, ethics, and metaphysics. A number of his essays have been collected in *The Virtue of Faith and Other Essays* (New York: Oxford University Press, 1987), and he will soon publish a major study of the philosophy of Leibniz.

William P. Alston is professor of philosophy at Syracuse University. He has written extensively in philosophy of religion, philosophy of language, and epistemology. His most recent books include *Divine Nature and Human Language* (Ithaca, N.Y.: Cornell University Press, 1989), *Epistemic Justification* (Ithaca, N.Y.: Cornell University Press, 1989), and *Perceiving God* (Ithaca, N.Y.: Cornell University Press, 1991).

David B. Burrell, C.S.C., is Theodore M. Hesburgh Professor in the Departments of Theology and Philosophy at the University of Notre Dame. His scholarship ranges over topics in medieval and modern religious thought and in the philosophy of language. His recent works include *Aquinas: God and Action* (Notre Dame, Ind.: University of Notre Dame Press, 1979), *Knowing the Unknowable God* (Notre Dame, Ind.: University of Notre Dame Press, 1986), and *Freedom and Creation in Three Traditions* (Notre Dame, Ind.: University of Notre Dame Press, 1993).

James M. Gustafson is Henry Luce Professor of Humanities and Comparative Studies at Emory University. He was formerly professor of theological ethics at the University of Chicago Divinity School, and his writings in that field include *Can Ethics Be Christian?* (Chicago: University of Chicago Press, 1975), *Protestant and Roman Catholic Ethics* (Chicago: University of Chicago Press, 1978), and *Ethics from a Theocentric Perspective* (Chicago: University of Chicago Press, 1981, 1984), vols. 1 and 2.

William Hasker is professor of philosophy at Huntington College. He has written numerous essays on topics in philosophy of religion and metaphysics. His writings include *Metaphysics* (Downers Grove, Ill.: InterVarsity Press, 1983) and a study of divine foreknowledge and human freedom titled *God, Time, and Knowledge* (Ithaca, N.Y.: Cornell University Press, 1989).

Kathryn E. Tanner is associate professor of Religious Studies at Yale University. She writes on topics in historical and contemporary theology. Her published work includes *God and Creation in Christian Theology* (Oxford: Basil Blackwell, 1988) and a recent discussion of theology and politics titled *The Politics of God* (Philadelphia: Augsburg Fortress, 1992).

Thomas F. Tracy is professor in the Department of Philosophy and Religion at Bates College. His writings include studies of divine action and the problem of evil. He is the author of *God, Action, and Embodiment* (Grand Rapids, Mich.: William B. Eerdmans, 1984).

Maurice Wiles is Regius Professor of Divinity Emeritus, Christ Church, Oxford. He has contributed extensively to discussions of the development of Christian doctrine and its revision in contemporary theology. His writings include *The Making of Christian Doctrine* (London: Cambridge University Press, 1967), *The Remaking of Christian Doctrine* (Philadelphia: Westminster Press, 1978), *Faith and the Mystery of God* (Philadelphia: Fortress Press, 1982), and *God's Action in the World* (London: SCM Press, 1986).

INTRODUCTION

Thomas F. Tracy

The affirmation that God acts in history has deep roots in the religious traditions of the West. As Judaism and Christianity took shape, they collected a rich body of stories about God's dealings with humanity, and these stories profoundly formed the religious life and theological imagination of the communities that preserved them as Scripture. The God identified and proclaimed in the biblical narratives is by no means a detached spectator of the great and tragic events of history. Rather, God engages human beings in and through their history, shaping the destinies of individuals and communities. So, the biblical stories tell of a God who enters into a covenant relationship with Abraham and his descendants, seals that covenant by liberating the Hebrew people from bondage in Egypt and giving them the law at Sinai, judges and redeems the community in its history of triumphs and defeats, raises up kings and prophets, and so on. And in the astonishing Christian telling of the culmination of this tale, God enters history in a particular individual to bring the divine-human relationship to fulfillment. The biblical stories, in short, depict God as one who calls us and our world into being for the sake of an unfolding relationship that is renewed by ongoing divine action in history and fulfilled through God's sovereign loving-kindness.

We are not entitled, of course, to move directly from noting the canonical status of these stories to the conclusion that some particular account of divine action is essential to Jewish or Christian theology. The stories can be read in more than one way, and theologians (especially in the modern era) have worried at length about the hermeneutical issues involved in the transition from story to theology. Furthermore, the biblical materials include images of God other than that of a transcendent personal agent and genres of literature other than narrative. Nonetheless, the idea that God acts in the world is sufficiently prominent in the texts and liturgical traditions of the biblical religions that any developed interpretation of their content must give some account of this persistent theme.

Not surprisingly, the significance of this topic is matched by its difficulty. While the stories about God's actions of judgment and mercy continue to shape the practice of religious life, the idea of divine action in the world has become a source of persistent puzzlement in contemporary theology. The history of these modern misgivings is too long to tell here, but it is worth briefly noting three overlapping sets of considerations that have contributed to the problematic status of the idea of a divine act.

First, the rise of the natural sciences demonstrated the power of understanding the world as a natural order in which events can be explained by their intelligible relation to other natural events, without reference to supernatural agencies. As the new sciences developed, they progressively rid themselves of theological entanglements, finding that their particular explanatory purposes could best be served without making appeal to divine action. Theologians were left to puzzle out the relation between scientific descriptions of the world as a law-governed structure and religious affirmations about history as the scene of divine action. If the world is understood as a closed causal system, as it was widely taken to be throughout the eighteenth and nineteenth centuries, then divine action appears to be restricted to ordering that system initially in creation and intervening within it later on in miracle.

Second, modern critical examination of the Bible increasingly drove a wedge between the biblical stories and scholarly history. Accounts of miracles came in for special critical scrutiny and skepticism. But if one doubts the historicity of, say, the specific miracles related in the story of the Exodus, then in what way is God an agent (or *the* agent) of these events; if God did not bring about plagues, parted waters, and pillars of fire and cloud, then what *did* God do in order to free the Hebrew people from their Egyptian bondage? Once it is granted that biblical narratives cannot be read as straightforward reports of God's deeds, we must grapple with the question of how they should be understood and, in particular, what claims they warrant about divine action in the world.[1]

Third, at least since the Enlightenment, theologians have worried about a powerful set of religious and ethical objections to the idea that God performs particular actions in history. Some of the actions attributed to God (by the biblical writers as well as by later religious thinkers) strike modern moral sensibilities as problematic in a number of ways: they may reflect the hostilities or self-interest of a particular group, they seem to involve favoritism and injustice, and so on. Furthermore, the general problem of evil arises here with great poignancy and power. If God's will is sovereign over human history, then why is that history so full of sorrow and destruction? If God does act in the world to direct events toward the fulfillment of the divine purposes, then why does God not do so to better effect?

These modern misgivings about the idea of divine action set the context for the conversation between theologians and philosophers that unfolds in this collection of essays. The last twenty years have seen a remarkable resurgence of philosophical interest in topics that have their home within the theistic religious traditions of the West. Philosophy of religion has shaken off the preoccupation with logical positivism and the hostility to metaphysical reflection that so dominated its attention and constricted its imagination a generation ago. This renewed vitality extends not only to the classical debates over the existence of God and the problem of evil. Philosophers working in a broadly analytic mode now regularly discuss such topics as divine eternity, foreknowledge and human freedom, and the nature of faith. Perhaps the most striking recent development is the readiness of philosophers to move beyond the analysis of a generic theism-in-general to consider specifically Christian concepts and doctrines such as divine incarnation, atonement, trinity, sin, and salvation. Here philosophers step onto the traditional territory of theology; in so doing they sometimes see themselves as reinhabiting positions largely

---

1. This is the problem that Langdon Gilkey pressed so effectively against the "Biblical theologians." See Gilkey's "Cosmology, Ontology, and the Travail of Biblical Language," *Journal of Religion* 41 (1961): 194–205. On biblical theology see, for example, G. Ernest Wright, *God Who Acts: Biblical Theology as Recital* (London: SCM, 1952), and G. Ernest Wright and Reginald H. Fuller, *The Book of the Acts of God* (Garden City, N.Y.: Doubleday, 1957). The title of this anthology, of course, echoes that of Wright's manifesto for the biblical theology movement.

abandoned by post-Enlightenment theologians,[2] who have (on this view) conceded too much to the "cultured despisers of religion." For anyone who is familiar with the debates of an earlier generation over the alleged cognitive meaninglessness of theological language,[3] it is a remarkable turn of events to find prominent philosophers chiding theologians for not being bold enough in their affirmations.

Clearly the time is right for an expanded conversation between philosophers and theologians on a range of topics in religious thought that are of great importance and mutual interest. This volume is designed to foster such a conversation by bringing together a number of prominent contributors in these fields and inviting them to think through the issues surrounding the claim that God acts in history. The discussion includes essays by both theologians and philosophers, and a response is given to each essay by a representative of the *other* discipline.

The essays and responses form a closely integrated exchange of views that is organized into two parts. The chapters in Part I take up a set of crucial questions about particular divine action and the problem of evil.

Maurice Wiles opens the discussion by pressing the case for a theology that sharply limits claims about God's activity in the world. As we noted above, it has become commonplace in modern theology to contend that the idea of particular divine action runs afoul of scientific expectations about the order and regularity of our world. Wiles shares this view, and contends that the findings and underlying presuppositions of the natural sciences impose fundamental constraints on the claims that we can make about God's activity in the world. He goes on to argue, however, that over and above this external scientific critique, there are specifically *religious* grounds for abandoning talk of special divine acts. Even if the notion of divine intervention could be salvaged from the skepticism inspired by modern science, there are nonetheless moral considerations *internal* to Christian theology that provide powerful reasons to reject it. Indeed, far from being imposed on theology from the outside, this critical rethinking can be found even within the biblical roots of the tradition, where earlier accounts of God's deeds are reassessed in light of later understandings

2. Thomas Morris, for example, describes the recent work of philosophers of religion in this way. See his introduction to *Philosophy and the Christian Faith*, ed. T. Morris (Notre Dame, Ind.: University of Notre Dame Press, 1988). The essays in Morris's volume nicely illustrate the development of a new philosophical theology.

3. See, for example, the famous "University Discussion," in *New Essays in Philosophical Theology*, ed. Antony Flew and Alasdair MacIntyre (London: SCM, 1955).

of the moral goodness of God. Wiles insists that this process of criticism and revision must continue; we too must ask whether familiar scriptural and theological depictions of God's acts are morally acceptable. If it is said that God sometimes performs particular actions in nature and history, then we must candidly confront the moral objections associated with the problem of evil: for example, is it consistent with God's beneficence or fairness to intervene so as to spare one innocent person while permitting many others to perish? It is best, Wiles contends, to deny altogether that God initiates and directs specific events, and to think instead of a continuous divine creative activity that establishes the overall direction of the world's history but that leaves the details up to God's free creatures. On this account, it is still possible to identify particular events as God's acts insofar as they especially advance God's overall purposes. It is necessary, however, to reject or revise a number of traditional Christian claims that presuppose divine intervention (most notably, claims about the physical resurrection of Jesus).

In response to Maurice Wiles, Robert Adams argues that the idea of particular divine action should continue to play a role in theology, and he does so by considering precisely the problem that crucially motivates Wiles's theological revisions, namely, the problem of evil. If a free will theodicy is to be morally plausible, Adams contends, the good for the sake of which God permits freedom (and therefore moral evil) must be something richer than simply the free exercise of moral virtue. The horrors made possible by human freedom appear too great and the moral goods achieved too uncertain for this alone to bear the weight of theodicy. Most theists have held that the good which God intends for us consists in personal relationship with God, a relationship that is brought to fulfillment in a life beyond death. This is a good that includes, but vastly exceeds, the value of moral virtue, and life after death provides a larger context for the fulfillment of God's purposes. In making such a life available to us, it appears that God acts outside the ordinary course of nature; that is, miraculously, as Christians have affirmed God did in raising Jesus from the dead. If this lies at the heart of Christian theodicy, then there is also a place for occasional miracles in this life, namely, to anticipate the reality that is to come and to convey God's special concern for us as individuals. In these events God acts a loving parent or friend, rather than as an impersonally equitable cosmic bureaucrat.

William Alston continues the discussion of particular divine action, defending this idea against a series of objections, including those raised by Maurice Wiles. Alston focuses on the claim that God not only creates and sustains the world as a whole, but also acts *in response* to human actions. In doing so, God plays a role within the world's unfolding history, bringing about particular events (which otherwise would not have occurred) in order to further the divine purposes. Alston explicitly replies to the charge that direct divine action of this sort is ruled out by the findings and/or methods of the modern sciences. We should not assume the truth of universal causal determinism, and we need not think of divine actions as "violations" of the laws of nature. As Wiles's essay has made clear, however, there are also theological objections to the idea that God acts amid created causes to bring about particular events in history, and Alston briefly replies to three of them. The first is the charge that this idea diminishes God by making the divine agent just one actor among others, all of whom contend for causal influence on the same level. The second theological worry, which Alston draws from Wiles, is that divine interventions in history would interfere with human freedom. The third and most compelling objection concerns the problem of evil and the apparent partiality of providence. This, Alston grants, is a substantial difficulty, but he contends that it is just as serious a problem for Wiles's "noninterventionist" position as for his own, and so it does not provide grounds for deciding between them. He concludes with a critical examination of Wiles's revisionist proposal that we should think of God as acting *solely* by creating and sustaining a world whose history is constrained by God's founding purposes.

James Gustafson challenges Alston's claim that the idea of particular divine action lies at the heart of Christianity. The conception of God as a personal agent is but one of the ways of speaking of the divine that can claim support in Scripture, in theological tradition, and in religious experience. Gustafson briefly surveys each of these sources of theological authority, and he concludes that they provide good grounds for a significantly different way of thinking about God: namely, as impersonal numinous cosmic power and order. This view, he contends, cannot be said to step entirely outside the Christian tradition, precisely because that tradition is not so unified in its conception of God as Alston suggests. Gustafson goes on to sketch some of the considerations that favor a break with, or at least a profound qualification of, the personal agency model in theology. These include the charge that this model is excessively anthropocentric, that it faces special difficulties in responding to the problem of evil, that it bears an uneasy relation to modern scientific understandings of the world, and that it is tied to certain problematic tendencies in Christian ethics.

In Part II, the center of attention shifts a bit. The discussion thus far has focused principally upon the claim that God performs certain special actions at particular times and places, actions that advance God's purposes in a way that goes beyond establishing and preserving the world as a whole. Now the discussion broadens to explore God's relation to the course of ordinary events: that is, events in which creatures exercise the powers of action that God has given them. Can we say that, quite apart from any "intervention" or "miracle," God acts in and through the processes of nature and history? And if we do make a claim of this kind, do we face a renewed problem about God's relation to evil?

In my own contribution to this volume, I explore whether and how it might be claimed that the activity of creatures is also the action of God, so that a single event can be attributed *both* to God's agency *and* to a natural cause or free human agent. This claim at least appears to hold out the prospect of resolving problems about divine action and the order of nature, on the one hand, and about divine grace and human freedom, on the other. But can this idea of "double agency," as Austin Farrer termed it, be developed coherently?[4] Farrer held that the coincidence of divine and created agencies constitutes an unanalyzable paradox that we can only partially illuminate with carefully qualified analogies. I argue, however, that while there are profound conceptual and epistemic limits on what we can say about God's agency, these limits do not warrant an appeal to paradox. The task of explication remains, and so I turn to a recent proposal by Kathryn Tanner that claims to establish the coherence of a particularly strong form of double agency.[5] She argues that the doctrine of creation requires that God be the total and immediate cause of every finite event. Her account runs into fundamental difficulties, however, in trying to show the consistency of this claim with the affirmations that (a) created things possess and exercise causal powers of their own and (b) human beings sometimes act freely. I consider each of these difficulties with her position, and I develop an alternative account of the ways in which God can be understood to act through the activity of natural causes and free human agents. Although we cannot say that our free

4. See *Faith and Speculation* (New York: New York University Press, 1967), v.
5. *God and Creation in Christian Theology* (Oxford: Basil Blackwell, 1988).

acts are direct acts of God, there are nonetheless several theologically significant senses in which we can speak of double agency.

David Burrell's response draws on his own long reflection on these issues to suggest a way of thinking about God's relation to created agents that is in substantial agreement with Tanner's views. The affirmation that God is the free creator of the world decisively sets the context for talk of divine and created agencies. God's action toward creatures is always that of causing their existence, and the existence God gives them is one in which they too share in "the dignity of causing." Burrell emphasizes that, in reflecting on this universal divine action, it is crucial to appreciate the full significance of the radical difference between creator and creature. God and creatures do not belong to any common genus as agents or even as beings, and in speaking of God as creative agent, we are putting the language of action to a use whose rules "are quite unknown to us." As a result, when we say that God wills that a person perform a particular action, we should not conclude that this necessitates that the person perform the action, and therefore that the person was not free in doing so. God causes the existence of the person-acting-freely, but this is a unique relation; it does not carry with it the entailments that we are familiar with in our talk of the acts of finite agents. Rather, if we remember the different ways in which language is used of creator and creature, we will say that both God as creator and the finite person as free agent are each, "in their respective domains," the total cause of the latter's act.

Kathryn Tanner's paper offers an energetic defense of her understanding of God's action as creator in the activity of each creature. If we take the idea of creation with full seriousness, she contends, we must say that all creatures, in all aspects of their being and operation that are good, depend directly upon God's continuous creative activity. It follows that every event in the world (again, insofar as it is good) is God's act. Note that this position, like that of Maurice Wiles, interprets the idea of providence exclusively in terms of God's ongoing creative activity. But in Tanner's account, God does not (as it were) stand at a distance from the world and carry out a policy of nonintervention. Rather, the reason God cannot be said to "intervene" is precisely because God is already the direct agent of every created event. Further, this sovereign divine agency necessarily achieves what it intends.

Tanner is well aware that these claims might be thought to conflict with certain widely held views about natural causation and human freedom, and she deploys a network of arguments in reply, relying crucially upon a distinction between the levels on which God and creatures act. She concludes that her understanding of divine action is compatible with even the strongest libertarian accounts of human freedom within the created order, but that we must not claim that created agents are free in their "vertical" relation to God; we "*must* choose when and what God wills." Human beings, however, sometimes make morally wrong choices, and so there arises here a particularly forceful version of the problem of evil. Sin results from a defective act of will that reflects a failure of attention. This defective action, Tanner grants, must be attributed to human freedom and is *not* willed by God. Sin, therefore, constitutes an exception to the principle that nothing can occur outside the creative will of God, and so sin is an inexplicable surd, an "impossible possibility."

William Hasker, in contrast to David Burrell, reads Tanner as advancing a form of theological determinism. He replies to her position from the point of view of theological libertarianism: that is, as one who affirms that if a human choice is free, it cannot be determined by any natural cause or intentional agent (including God) other than the chooser herself. If this is what freedom entails, then Tanner's position cannot rightly be said to accommodate free human choice, even though it allows for human actions that are not determined by any *created* cause or agent. The central objection to theological determinism, as we have seen, is that it generates an intractable problem about God's relation to evil. Hasker examines Tanner's reply to this problem, and he argues that her efforts to resolve it lead her back to an assertion of precisely the freedom she initially denied, namely, a human freedom to act against the will of God.

These essays vividly reflect the interplay of competing concerns and strategies in contemporary thought about the God Who Acts. The issues that have driven modern reconsideration of this subject are much in evidence here, and they are subtly interconnected in the essayists' positions. Questions about theology and science, about emphasis and interpretation in the use of biblical materials, and about the problem of evil interact in shaping these proposals and in framing critical challenges to them. In addition, the discussion often hinges on both fundamental questions concerning the concepts of causality and free agency and subtle judgments about the powers and limits of theological language. The authors' decisions about these underlying conceptual and metaphysical issues shape their assessments of what is possible in theological reflection upon divine action in the world.

The exchange of views that develops in response to these questions gives ample evidence of the renewed vitality of philosophical theology. No longer are philosophers principally in the role of skeptical outsiders; they speak here on behalf of the theological traditions under discussion. Indeed, in the first pair of essays and responses, it is the theologians who argue the dubiousness of certain familiar ways of speaking about divine action and the philosophers who offer a defense. At the same time, the theologians call attention to the internal variety and richness of the theological tradition and to the need for detailed appreciation of the textual and historical sources of Christian thought. It quickly becomes apparent here that lines of convergence and divergence among the views of these authors cut across disciplinary boundaries. Philosophers and theologians now find themselves talking about many of the same issues, though they do so in largely distinct networks of discussion and with rather different frames of reference. Clearly, they have a great deal to contribute to each other.

This volume brings a small selection of contributors to these fields into a shared circle of conversation. It will take an ongoing effort to sustain and expand this kind of exchange, so that philosophers and theologians become increasingly familiar with each other's literatures, characteristic concerns, and habits of thought. The liveliness of the discussion conducted in these pages, however, suggests that this effort will be well worth making.

PART I

PARTICULAR DIVINE ACTION: PROVIDENCE AND THE PROBLEM OF EVIL

CHAPTER 1

DIVINE ACTION: SOME MORAL CONSIDERATIONS[1]

Maurice Wiles

God's action in history is a fundamental feature of Christian faith, but there are serious puzzles as to how such action is to be understood. The God with whom we are concerned is not just any one of the "Gods many and Lords many" (to use Paul's phrase) who populated the ancient world. It is the transcendent God of Christian faith who creates *ex nihilo,* who is, that is to say, the ultimate source of all that is. Any account we give of God's acting in history is bound to be closely correlated with our understanding of his broader relation with the natural world. We may separate our study of history in the humanities from our study of the physical world in the natural sciences, but the separation is artificial. The history in which God is affirmed to act is a history of embodied persons living in a physical world. So we need to be as clear as we can about our general

---

1. I am grateful to my colleagues, John Fenton and Arthur Peacocke, for helpful comments on an earlier draft of this essay.

understanding of God's relation to the created order, before we embark on our reflections about the nature of God's specific actions in history. How can a necessary and eternal God create a contingent and temporal world? How can he sustain the world and its laws of operation in being? How can he influence particular occurrences within it? These are important preliminary questions before we come to deal directly with the question, How can God act in history?

I have posed those questions in a particular form that seems a natural enough way of putting the kind of difficulty that imposes itself upon us. But questions beginning "How can . . ." may be of very different kinds and require very different kinds of answers. I want, therefore, to differentiate three such types as a first step toward clarifying what kind of an answer might be appropriate in the case of these theological questions.

1. *How can a magnet make iron filings jump?* The question expresses a puzzlement in need of resolution, because metal objects in close proximity to one another don't usually generate movement like that. The way to answer the question and remove the sense of puzzlement is to analyze the physical properties of the objects concerned and set out the physical laws in accordance with which the iron filings move as they do. That kind of model needs to be eschewed altogether in the theological case. We are not looking for some law that governs the way in which God sustains the laws of the universe in operation. That would be to turn the theological question into a scientific question, and to cease to talk appropriately about God. But the model could mislead us in another, more subtle way. We have independent access to the magnet and to the iron filings. We can deal with each in isolation from the other, analyze their properties separately, and thereby further our understanding of how they relate to one another. We cannot do that in the case of God and the universe, though we often talk as if we could. We do not know that God is eternal independently of our knowledge of the universe as having a beginning (if indeed we can rightly be said to know that), in such a way that we could analyze each separately and then see how the notions might fit together. Rather, God is our symbol for that which underlies, gives existence to and makes sense of our finite and temporal existence. His "eternity" is only known to us as the ground of that which has a beginning. Our puzzlement about how an eternal God can create the beginning is not like our puzzlement about the magnet. To treat it as if it were can generate a style of discussion of divine attributes (as truths about God known indepen-

dently of any knowledge about the world) that is inconsistent with the way in which the concept of God is grounded.

2. *How can I move my arm at will?* There is both similarity and difference here in relation to our first example. The experience is so common that the sense of puzzlement does not arise without a fairly sophisticated process of reflection. Physical movement is normally the result of identifiable physical causes, and follows some predictably regular pattern. But in this case it seems to be a mental act of willing that gives rise to the physical movement, and in a way that makes it very hard for the observer to predict. We may start by trying to deal with the problem in the same way as we dealt with the initially problematic character of the magnet's behavior; that is, by seeking to reveal some initially hidden aspects of the physical movement through neurological studies of the brain. But the fundamentally problematic character of the mind-body relation remains untouched. Philosophy seeks to deal with the question by a process of redefinition. It develops ways of speaking about "intentions" and about "basic actions," which enable us to talk about our common experience of the willed movement of our own bodies in a way that minimizes (though it does not altogether remove) the sense of strangeness implicit in talk of mental acts causing physical movements. This offers a rather better guide for the strategy appropriate to answering questions about how God can create and sustain the world in being. In both cases—the experience of the willed movement of our bodies and the conviction that the underlying dynamism of the world derives from God—we are dealing not with occasional or unusual phenomena but with something basic to our experience. Yet in both cases the ways in which it is most natural and customary to articulate that basic phenomenon are in *prima facie* conflict with the ordinary usage of our language in relation to everything else. So attempts at redefinition, adjustments to the way in which we describe this basic, but apparently anomalous, feature of our experience seem to be a reasonable ploy. Thus in the theological case we mix the more traditional language of the craftsman with that of the world as God's body or God as author, playwright, or composer. None succeeds in removing altogether the puzzlement that gave rise to the question, but in suitable combination they may offer some alleviation from the sense of puzzlement engendered by other formulations or by each formulation on its own.

3. *How can a parent batter his or her child to death?* This is a very different kind of question. No puzzlement of the kind present in the first

two cases is involved. There is no mystery about the means by which the parent causes the death. It is rather a cry of moral incomprehension. On the basis of our normal experience, we find it difficult to conceive how the widely felt ties of natural affection and the demands of moral responsibility could be so completely overridden. Any answer to our question will have to take the form of a deeper recognition of the potentially radical character of human evil, a new understanding of the results of drug addiction and consideration of any other such factors that may be relevant to the particular case. In discussion between philosophers and theologians about the nature of divine agency, we would expect to find reference to metaphysics, philosophy of science, philosophy of history, and philosophy of mind. Moral philosophy might not at first seem so obvious a candidate for inclusion in that list. Yet this third example suggests another and perfectly proper sense to the words: How can God create? How can God create a universe, that appears to be built not just on the unavenged tears of Dostoyevsky's one innocent child, but on those of countless innocents: children, women, and men? Most of us, I suspect, are likely to adopt some form of the free-will defense in answering such a question—once again not in the expectation of removing the sense of puzzlement altogether but as a way of mitigating its more vertiginous forms. Again, it is not my intention to consider the various arguments for and against the free-will defense in this essay. But I believe, as I shall be arguing more fully a little later on, that the inclusion of this moral dimension in our considerations is a matter of the greatest importance.

Keeping these preliminary reflections in mind, let us approach our more specific question: How can God act in history? Once again we have to be on our guard against a possible danger of posing the question that way. We do not have a prior knowledge of God as agent in history, independent of all ideas about the possible nature of such agency. Any notion of divine agency will have grown out of some purported apprehension of God in history, and the notion can never, therefore, be wholly neutral in relation to what kind of form it might take.

Some theologians would want to put the point a good deal more sharply. Those whose approach to theology has been strongly influenced by Karl Barth or whose approach falls under the umbrella title of "Narrative Theology" are inclined to claim that, for the Christian, God is exclusively defined by the stories of his dealings with the world as given in Scripture. For them there is no generic "concept of divine agency"; there is only the God whose acts are made known to us through the biblical narrative. An extreme approach of that kind seems to me to be beset by major and insuperable problems. It is not at all clear (as I shall be developing more fully later) that there is one biblical narrative disclosing the identity of the only true God, the biblical "God Who Acts." Nor, even if that difficulty could be overcome more successfully than I believe it can, would it rule out altogether the propriety of the kind of question being raised in this essay. Neither the philosophical inquiry nor the elucidation of the identity of the God of the Bible can be carried through independently of the other. Interaction between the two is not a further refinement to be pursued by specialists on the philosophico-theological frontier, after their essential work as either philosopher or theologian has already been brought to completion. Any serious engagement with the subject must be open to the changing insights of both disciplines at the same time.

In seeking now to give a little more precision to the appropriate kind of cooperation between philosophers and theologians, let me begin by trying to articulate a way in which the problem is often approached but which seems to me to fall short of the kind of interrelation between the two disciplines that is really required. The biblical story, it is often said, and the subsequent Christian doctrine of providence posit divine agency as something fundamental to the claims they want to make. We have to acknowledge that those claims cannot be sustained in all the forms in which the Bible and traditional doctrine present them. The difficulties that rightly hold us back from doing so are not entirely new. They have often been recognized and taken seriously in the past. But they do impinge on us with a genuinely new force, particularly as a result of the perceived regularities in nature that have made possible progress in scientific understanding. Those difficulties do not only impinge on people who hold a mechanistic or physically deterministic view of the universe. We could be shot of them easily enough if that were the case, since scientific and philosophical study combine to show such a view of the universe to be false. But the ideas of divine intervention of the kind portrayed in the Bible and assumed in much past Christian writing about providence come into conflict also with the well-tested working assumptions of regularity and uniformity on which the scientific enterprise is based. Those assumptions do not rule out the idea of divine agency as such. Let us, therefore, it may be said, see what conception of God's action is allowed by the philosopher to be both internally coherent and compatible with our present knowledge and ways of acquiring knowledge about the world. And let us with gratitude accept that conception as one that enables us to be true to the basic insights of our faith and at the same time hold to that faith with integrity and not in some kind of schizophrenic relation to our modern, scientific understanding of the world.

Such an approach is right to insist that the implications of our modern understanding of the world and philosophical reflection about that understanding need to be taken very seriously into account by the theologian. Nevertheless it seems to do so in too passive a way. The faith ought not to be thought of in terms of a series of biblical utterances or dogmatic formulas, whose meaning and intelligibility it is left to the philosopher to elucidate. The raw material of Christian theology is far less fixed than such a picture suggests. The Bible itself, and the subsequent history of Christian thought, reveal a much more open attempt to make sense of and live by the foundation experiences to which Scripture bears witness. The theologian must be in on the action of determining how divine agency is appropriately to be understood, and ought not to commit him- or herself in advance to the view that if the ideas of divine intervention and of miracle are found to be philosophically viable, then they are of course to be welcomed and endorsed by the theologian. Religious reasons do not all necessarily point in favor of such ideas. There may, indeed, be specifically religious reasons against them.

It is not only the case that Scripture does not hold a uniform view of divine action. We can see changes actually taking place, with later writers repudiating the view of their predecessors. Let me take an example. 2 Samuel 24 recounts a story of how "the Lord gave David orders that Israel and Judah should be counted." David does what he is told, and as a result of his obedience incurs the Lord's anger and has to choose among three years of famine, three months of military defeat, and three days of pestilence. The story, like most of the stories in the books of Samuel and Kings, is repeated in the later books of Chronicles, specifically in 1 Chronicles 21. But, as is regularly the case, the story is told with a difference. The story begins: "Now Satan . . . incited David to count the people." The change is not the outcome of new revelation by subsequent intervention of God; it was not due to the appearance of some new angelic press officer from the courts of heaven, announcing, in the spirit of the days of Watergate, that the earlier revelation was at fault and God had not himself authorized the instructions given to David. No, it is a matter of changed theological and moral convictions on the part of the author. In the later period of the Old Testament history many writers are reluctant, for reasons of reverence, even to name the name of God; they prefer to use more indirect periphrases and tend to ascribe even the most beneficent activity within the world to some angelic figure rather than directly to God himself as earlier writers had done. That motive is undoubtedly at work here too. But most commentators are agreed that changed moral convictions are also a part of the story. The later writer "desires to remove the offence caused by the statement that Yahweh was the direct instigator of an act portrayed as sinful"; "he cannot in his time attribute the source of evil to God."[2] So it is by a process of moral criticism that the earlier account of God's action is denied, and a new one substituted in its place. What the Chronicler provides is admittedly only a slight amelioration of the problem. It is unlikely that he sees Satan as the unqualified adversary in bitter conflict with God (as under the influence of Persian dualism Satan came to be regarded in the Book of Revelation and in so much subsequent Christian history). His role here is almost certainly closer to that of the Satan who appears in the prose opening of the Book of Job, a divine courtier whose work of tempting human persons is carried out with explicit divine permission. Nevertheless the main point stands. What we see going on is a process of moral criticism functioning as a vital factor in determining how God's action is to be understood. Moreover, that process is not one that is achieved and finished once and for all. As the not unambiguous form of the resolution of the problem in the second story reveals, it is a process that has to go on.

That same process can be seen at work in changing attitudes within Scripture to natural disasters both personal and corporate. The Psalmist has never seen a righteous man forsaken or his children begging for bread (Ps. 37:25); but determination to see all misfortune as God-given in that morally appropriate way leads to gross misrepresentation of the human moral evidence, as by Job's friends, whose views receive short shrift from God in the final section of the book. And in Saint John's gospel the disciples are told that the reason for the blindness of the man born blind has nothing to do either with his sin or even with that of his parents (John 9:1–3). In the more public sphere, it was, the Genesis writer tells us, the Lord who rained down fire and brimstone on Sodom and Gomorrah (Gen. 19:24) and he would not have done so had there been ten righteous persons there (nor, indeed, one must presume, had there been one righteous person, but Abraham could not pluck up his courage to go that far); but that understanding of natural disaster is denied by the gospel when we

2. E. L. Curtis, *I.C.C. Commentary*, ad loc.; J. M. Myers, *Anchor Bible Commentary*, ad loc.

are told that there was nothing especially wicked about the eighteen people on whom the tower of Siloam fell (Luke 13:4–5). The moral facts of the universe do not allow us to continue to regard natural phenomena as specifically directed actions of God in the way that the early biblical stories do. But once again, though the problem may be eased, it is not solved. God is not the determining cause of the man's blindness or the tower's collapse for moral reasons associated with the particular people involved. But the possibility of his still being cause of the event is not explicitly denied. It is rather that the importance of the question of causality is being downgraded. The alternatives suggested in the text are of a different order—teleological and deterrent in nature: the man was born blind "so that God's power might be displayed in curing him"; the fall of the tower is to prompt the reflection that "unless you repent, you will all of you come to the same end." Do these alternative types of explanation rule out any further inquiry about God's action in the world in a causal or interventionist sense? It does not seem to me that they do. They may well raise the question whether the issue of causality is the most important issue religiously; and they may also warn us how difficult it is likely to be to find a satisfactory answer. But neither of those considerations rules out the propriety of the inquiry. What the cases we have been considering reveal is a process of modification, within the course of the period covered by the biblical writings, of how God's action is to be understood, arising out of moral reflection—in this case, reflection on the moral status of the human persons involved. And once again we have not reached a point of equilibrium. Puzzlement remains that cries out for further critical reflection.

So far the examples I have taken have been of ostensibly evil happenings, where the relation of God to the initiation of the events in question is bound to be problematic. As a final example from the biblical narratives, I want to take a New Testament incident of apparently unmitigated providential benefit. The Matthaean birth stories tell of a warning given to Joseph in a dream that resulted in the escape of the Holy Family to Egypt and in the preservation of the infant Jesus from the murderous intentions of Herod. What could be more beneficial than the rescue of an innocent baby? What more providential than the survival of the Christ child? Here, it might seem, whatever other difficulties may have to be faced in accepting it as a story of a specific divine action, no moral difficulty of the kind I have been discussing need raise its head. But it does not take much reflection to realize that is not the case. Moral difficulties abound. If God warns through dreams, why only Joseph? Were the other children of Bethlehem dispensable? Dispensable to the God without whom not a sparrow falls to the ground and whose Christ declares that what is done to the least of his brethren is done to him? Traditional piety has seen the story in the context of divine agency, and done its best to do so in a positive light. The Church of England Prayer Book collect for Holy Innocents' day addresses God as "Almighty God, who . . . madest infants to glorify thee by their deaths." But how many of us can seriously identify ourselves with such a form of address? By human moral standards, let alone any special gospel standards, the action described in the story is an immoral action, using the Holy Innocents only as a means, and not as ends in themselves. The same moral criteria, which we have seen at work as a crucial learning factor within Scripture itself in the attempt to come to some understanding of God's acting in the world, call this apparently beneficial and providential action of God seriously into question.

Now the story is, in my view, a legend and not a piece of history. So, have I been making an unnecessary fuss about what is only an edifying tale? I think not. Because if it is an edifying tale, part of its edifying purpose is to reveal the nature of God's providential preparation for the coming of Christ and to assure his followers of that same continuing providential care. What my analysis of the story has been designed to suggest is that there is an inescapable shadow side to such providential care.

To put the point in modern terms, suppose that a person is prevented by measles or a traffic jam from boarding the plane on which he or she was booked. The plane crashes with the loss of the lives of everyone on board. His or her friends give thanks to God for such a providential escape. But a little reflection leads them to use "providential" in a highly reductionist sense. If measles or the traffic jam was God's means of ensuring their friend's safety, might not a more infectious strain or an even solider logjam of cars have saved others as well? Or if only one were to be prevented from reaching the plane in time, why not the pilot so that the plane could not fly at all? One person's providence is another's downfall.

But do acts of providential divine intervention necessarily have this morally invidious character? It may be claimed that the most important examples of such intervention—namely, the virginal conception and the physical resurrection of Christ—are free of such embarrassing implications. In terms of immediate implications, of the kind I have been drawing in my examples so far, that is perfectly true. But the process of moral reflection cannot be content to consider only the immediate and short-term implications. More wide-ranging reflection reveals a continuing difficulty.

At an earlier point in this paper I alluded to some form of the free-will defense as necessary if Christians are not to abandon altogether any attempt to correlate their belief in God with their recognition of evil in the world. The essence of that defense is that the purpose (or at least a major aspect of the purpose) of the world's creation is the emergence of free human spirits, and that the achievement of that purpose logically requires the occurrence of some forms of moral and natural evil. In one sense, but a trivial one, God "could" prevent such evil. But in a far more significant sense he "could not," because it would be inconsistent with the central purpose of the world's creation. Creation of the only kind we know involves a divine self-limitation. The concept of divine intervention clearly constitutes a qualification of the nature and extent of that divine self-limitation. The question I want to pose is whether it may not amount to an undermining of the essential point of divine self-limitation altogether. The point of divine self-limitation is the necessity, not only of the possibility of wrong choice, but also of a stable background where actions give rise to consequences that are not subverted by special divine actions changing the expected consequences in ways that reward the good and punish the evil.

Clearly divine intervention on a large scale would undermine the point of the creation as the free-will defense envisages it. If divine intervention were substantially restricted in its scope, the answer to the question I have posed is not so clear. The regularity of the world's normal working would still provide the stable background deemed necessary for the development of morally responsible personal lives. But what of the occasions of divine intervention? If some divine intervention is compatible with God's creation of a world of emerging human persons, moral questions about the nature of those interventions inevitably arise. The degree of divine intervention implicit not merely in the claims of contemporary faith-churches but also in those of mainline Christian accounts of historical and personal providence is not inconsiderable. More worryingly, in many cases the nature of such claimed interventions seems trivial when set in the context of Auschwitz and Hiroshima, which no providential action prevented. This line of moral criticism, which I have argued a Christian who takes the biblical witness seriously is bound to pursue, raises serious questions about the religious acceptability of even a limited concept of divine intervention. It is not so much a matter of the particular form of intervention claimed, which was the central issue in the critical reflections within Scripture itself. It is a matter rather of those many places where no claim can reasonably be made. In the language of Sherlock Holmes, the problem is that of the dog that did not bark in the night.

The case that I have been arguing is that there are significant moral reasons against accepting the idea of direct or special actions of God in history of a kind that might appropriately be described as a form of divine intervention. There are, of course, also metaphysical considerations that can be brought to suggest the incompatibility of a strong doctrine of God's transcendence and the idea of divine intervention. It is not possible in the compass of this essay to review those considerations, though I think they have considerable force. In neither case, admittedly, is the argument decisive or irrefutable, and the same is true of the two arguments taken together. But then we ought not to expect that kind of decisive proof in a theological argument of this nature. To expect it is a sign that it is not the God of Christian faith about whom the argument is being conducted. But though inevitably not decisive, the cumulative force of these two arguments seems to me very strong.

For a Christian who feels their force in this way, two further lines of argument need to be pursued. The first is to ask whether there is a non-interventionist way of understanding divine agency, in terms of which it is still possible to develop a reasonably traditional understanding of Christian faith. A good deal of biblical and traditional teaching about providence does certainly take that form. The standard biblical examples are Joseph's brethren selling him into Egypt and the devastation of Israel by Assyria, "the rod of God's anger." Their jealous and aggressive actions are understood as also God's actions, bringing about God's providentially intended ends. I do not intend to pursue this line of investigation very far for reasons that will soon become evident.

If "action" is understood in something like its normal sense of the intentional initiation of a pattern of events, this revised approach does not offer much alleviation from the difficulties we have been considering. Although the difficulties attending the notion of intervention as such are no longer a problem, the coherence of describing the same series of events as both a divine action and a human action are equally formidable. It is difficult to find a way of understanding them that does not turn Joseph's brothers and the Assyrian generals into puppets manipulated for his own ends by the divine puppet-master. But I do not want to pursue that particular, very familiar, difficulty any further now. I do, however, want to stress another problem, more germane to the central theme of this essay; namely, that this approach provides little alleviation of the moral difficulties I have been considering. Those difficulties take two forms. In the first instance, some of the human acts that are said to coincide with divine acts, as in the two biblical examples I have cited, are morally reprehensible acts. Just as it proved necessary to modify those Old Testament accounts that ascribed directly to God actions of a morally scandalous kind, so too it seems morally necessary to play down any straightforward identification of an act like that of Joseph's brothers with the action of God. But, second, we have to ask how it is that, if God is able to act providentially in this sort of way, without recourse to special intervention, history has still produced its Auschwitzes and its Hiroshimas. What God's hidden providential working has failed to avert still raises awkward questions on this revised understanding of divine agency. Finally, we have to recognize that any account for which this noninterventionist interpretation of divine agency is the only style of divine agency to be allowed will have grave difficulties in dealing with such traditionally central Christian claims as the virginal conception of Jesus and his physical resurrection. This line of argument, therefore, does little to ease the difficulties that we have encountered so far, despite raising other difficulties of its own and also having to accept a strongly revisionist account of Christian doctrine.

If we are going to accept some such revisionist account (as I believe we should), there is a second line of argument that is open to us to pursue. It involves insisting that the idea of particular divine actions within nature and history (whether conceived in an interventionist sense or not) can only be admitted in a highly Pickwickian sense. Such an admission ought not to be dismissed as improper out of hand. As my first theological teacher, Ian Ramsey, used to say: Much theological language is characterized by logical oddity. And there is something Pickwickian already about saying that it was not Joseph's brothers but God who sent him to Egypt (Gen. 45:8). But that is not a license for Pickwickianism of any kind. The argument that I want to put forward must justify itself by the criteria of logical and moral coherence, and also that of adequacy to the witness of Christian faith.

On the understanding that I am now proposing, there is one action of God that can be affirmed in a relatively straightforward sense: namely, the continuing process of the world's creation, for that is a sequence of events dependent on the purposive activity of God for its initiation and continued existence. I call it "a relatively straightforward sense," because there is no analogy within the world for any activity involving such absolute creativity as is being affirmed here. Any attempt to speak of the "how" of God's creative action can only be by way of a highly tentative form of imaginative construction.

By contrast any putative activity of God within nature or history will be interpreted in a much more indirect sense. Clearly, since the whole process of creation is being seen as God's act, all particular occurrences fall within the context of God's action. Those which Scripture or tradition have spoken of as God's acts in some more precise sense have certainly been understood to have been initiated or directed by God in some specific, even if often oblique, manner. But very often it has been the end accomplished that has been the point of primary significance. It is Joseph's achieved position in Egypt and his ability thereby to provide what is needed for the preservation of his father and his brothers that gives rise to talk of God having sent him there. It is the deserved devastation of Israel that leads the prophet to describe Assyria as "the rod of God's anger" and to affirm that it was God who sent the Assyrians on their destructive campaign against the country. If we judge ourselves unable to make acceptable sense in such cases of the first and most obvious aspect of a particular act of God—namely, its specific initiation and direction by God—no difficulty of comparable magnitude attends the second, and possibly more significant, aspect. It seems clear that some things that happen in the world are pleasing to God and fulfill his purposes in a way that others do not. We may not always be sure which they are, but we have various criteria, particularly our moral sense, to help us in the vital task of discrimination. My proposal, therefore, is that our inherited Christian language about particular acts of God is best understood, not in relation to divine initiation or direction, but of actions whose results further the overall intention of God in the creation of the world or, to put it in more temporal terms, his will for the world at a particular moment in the light of the way in which we have developed its potential up to that point.

That is a highly revisionist thesis, though I have tried to show that it has points of continuity as well as of discontinuity with the tradition. Its Achilles' heel is not so much its intelligibility as whether it can meet the second criterion of adequacy to the witness of Christian faith. To demonstrate that would be a vast undertaking that I can only deal with very sketchily in an essay whose main burden has been to try to show why someone might feel bound to adopt such a position. What I propose to do is to look briefly at four issues, all of which might seem to pose particular difficulties for the approach I have been outlining. Two of these, namely "miracle" and "revelation," are relatively general aspects of traditional Christian doctrine; the other two are of a more particular nature, the "virginal conception" and the "physical resurrection" of Jesus, to both of which I have made brief allusion earlier. All four seem to call for a very strong sense of divine action in history—indeed, with the possible exception of "revelation," it would seem to be a directly interventionist understanding that is required.

1. Miracle

Attempts have been made to give a wholly noninterventionist account of miracle, notably by Paul Tillich. For him it is the objective correlate of whatever is grasped by what he calls "ecstatic reason," a form of apprehension that exceeds the bounds of the normal subject-object structure of finite reason, but that is emphatically not irrational or antirational.[3] I think he is pointing to something religiously and theologically important in what he says, as I shall indicate more fully in a moment. Nevertheless I think it is semantically confusing to use the word "miracle" in this sense in theological discussion. We need a word for the concept of an event directly caused by God that conflicts with normally experienced regularities of the world's working, even if we decide that it is not only a null class but a logically incoherent concept. I would prefer to keep the word "miracle" for that concept and say that miracle, so understood, should have no place in Christian theology.

2. Revelation

The concept of revelation I would want to deal with rather differently. It does not seem to me to be so tightly tied to an interventionist view as the

3. P. Tillich, *Systematic Theology* (London: James Nisbet, 1953), 1:124 and 128.

concept of miracle. It is true that it has often been understood to involve the direct impartation by God of knowledge about himself, which could not conceivably have been known to us by any other means. Moreover, that way of understanding revelation has often been regarded as of the essence of its religious importance, on the ground that it provides the only possible escape from the impasse of the fruitless attempts of finite and sinful human beings to wrest knowledge of the mystery of God by their own puny efforts. Nevertheless I regard that as a distorted understanding of revelation, which is seriously called into question not only by the "how" questions of philosophical inquiry but also by the nature of the scriptural writings themselves.

Revelation is the process whereby the normally hidden reality of God becomes disclosed. That process is not just a matter of rational argumentation. Basic religious awareness has a more intuitive, directly given character about it. Its occurrence is certainly not unrelated to past reflective thought, and calls for subsequent reflection of the critical reason upon it as well. But in itself it is other than and distinguishable from the reasoning process. It is what is indicated by the not altogether happy phrase of Tillich to which I have already referred, namely "ecstatic reason." There is, that is to say, a form of human awareness that allows some access to the basically hidden and mysterious reality of God, with which we have to do in faith. Its content may be much more provisional and colored by contingent forms of human understanding than is claimed for revelation when it is conceived as given in more interventionist ways. But it has still a claim to the designation "revelation." And it is in many ways more congruous with the way in which the scriptural writings have come into existence than is the more interventionist view.

3. Virginal Conception

This doctrine has played a substantial part in the history of Christian faith and practice. Its defense today seems to come mainly from those who find it hard to acknowledge that the Church could have been in error in building so much on its presumed historical truth. But the way in which the story of it is told in the birth narratives of Matthew and Luke leaves little doubt in my mind of its legendary character. It is a result of the conviction that the whole life of Jesus is to be seen as the definitive "act of God," not a necessary reason for its being so nor a ground for its coming to be believed to be so.

4. The Physical Resurrection

In this case the issue is similar but by no means so straightforward. Some of the resurrection stories are certainly of a legendary character, as the birth narratives are. And some New Testament scholars argue that, as in the case of the virginal conception, so here the story of Jesus' bodily resurrection is a result of already established conviction about the significance of his life and death rather than a cause of that conviction. But there is a good deal of evidence that belief in the resurrection of Jesus in some sense was a part of the earliest apprehension and proclamation of his saving significance. The qualification I have introduced, "in some sense," is vital. It is certainly not clear that that earliest sense involved a physical, and in that sense unquestionably miraculous aspect. Certainly the early affirmations of the resurrection do not clearly distinguish it from the more theological concepts of divine vindication or exaltation to the right hand of God. My own view is that we simply do not have the appropriate evidence to determine with any confidence the nature of the immediate aftermath of the death of Jesus. Religiously, the doctrine expresses the conviction that the life and death of Jesus embody the divine purpose with transforming power, in a way that justifies our designation of them as "the act of God," in the sense in which I have suggested it is appropriate to understand that phrase. There are continuing puzzles in the proper understanding of resurrection, which cannot be pursued here. But I do not think that either the early New Testament witness to it or its role in Christian theology as a whole so clearly requires an interventionist understanding of divine action in relation to it, that it can function decisively against the general line of interpretation of divine agency that I am proposing.

Much more could be said on these issues if time and space allowed. And there are more issues at the heart of Christian theology, such as incarnation, grace, and intercessory prayer, that would call for similar critical reflection. But I hope I have said enough to suggest that the approach I have been putting forward should not be regarded as failing the adequacy criterion out of hand. So we ought, I believe, to be ready to follow the argument in the direction I am indicating, if the metaphysical arguments (which I have assumed rather than argued) and the moral arguments (which I have tried to develop in this essay) carry conviction. Both sets of arguments, in my judgment, are strong ones; their force in combination is formidable.

THEODICY AND DIVINE INTERVENTION

Robert Merrihew Adams

We are indebted to Maurice Wiles for a challenging, clearly argued essay. I want to say first of all that I am very much in agreement with his methodological remarks about the relation between philosophy and theology. It is certainly part of the business of a theologian to consider possibilities of revising theological views and formulations on the basis of *theological* or *religious* reasons, and not only on the basis of reasons arising from philosophy and other more or less secular disciplines. Theology done on behalf of a religious community is a discipline that has special reason to be respectful of traditions and texts that are seen by the community as playing a central role in its contact with God. But as a living discipline rooted in a living faith, theology must also insist on taking a fresh look at its sources and doctrines. Those who have devoted themselves comprehensively to the work of theology may be sensitive to reasons for revision that are apt to escape the notice of those of us who have specialized in some other discipline, such as philosophy.

In disagreeing, as I shall, with the particular revision of the conception of divine activity that Professor Wiles is proposing, I want therefore to take account of as wide a theological perspective as I can. Specifically, I shall be suggesting that theists who believe in a story of salvation will do well to try to relate that story as a whole to the issues before us. In effect, I shall be trying to outflank Wiles theologically—a maneuver that may well prove to be rash. He has based his argument on a problem very familiar to philosophers of religion, the problem of evil. But he has argued in a very interesting and persuasive way that this problem was already a basis in the composition of the Bible, in nonphilosophical contexts, for revisions of religious views. I begin my response to his argument with some reflections on a version of one of his biblical examples.

As I thought about what I should say in these comments there rose before my mind's eye the tormented faces of the people involved in the massacre of the Holy Innocents, as carved in high relief by Giovanni Pisano for the monumental pulpit of the church of Sant'Andrea in Pistoia, perhaps the most perfect surviving work of the greatest Italian sculptor of the Middle Ages. Visages of pain and panic grief; visages of cruelty, fear, and guilt; murdered babies: Why is this scene of horror selected to fill one of only five panels to tell the story of Christ? Was Giovanni a secret infidel, this carving his silent but eloquent cry of rage against the very idea of a creator? Probably not. And that surely was not the typical motivation of his contemporaries, who obviously thought the scene belonged in a cycle of representations of the life of Christ. It was not the motivation of the Franciscans, for instance, who had the slaughter of the innocents painted in the lower transept of their basilica in Assisi, with all the violence and passion, if not quite all the perfection, of Giovanni's masterpiece.

The murder of innocents by soldiers was only too familiar a fact of life to the people who made those images, and to those who paid for them and those who first contemplated them, as it is to great numbers of people in our own time, from Auschwitz to El Salvador and elsewhere. Perhaps the likeliest motive for selecting the Holy Innocents for inclusion in one's representation of the story of Christ is the desire to find some meaning for life's horrors by locating them in the context of a story of salvation. In Giovanni's carving in Pistoia there is a strong axis from lower left to upper right, most of the victims looking up, and Herod and most of the murderers looking down. The viewer's eye is drawn to follow the victims' gaze around the corner of the pulpit to the scene of the Crucifixion—

more suffering, but the suffering, this time, of God in the world, the body of Christ more serene, somehow, in its torment and its beauty. And the next and last panel presents the resurrection of all the dead, and the final judgment and righting of wrongs.

Many, perhaps all, of the Christians among us today would not choose to portray the story of Christ in exactly this way. Perhaps (for theological reasons indeed) we think that Giovanni's Last Judgment, like Michelangelo's in the Sistine Chapel, gives us too vindictive a picture of the victory of Christ. But the question I want to focus on now is whether it is a good idea to place the massacre of the Innocents in some such larger story. There is real controversy today, among religious people, over the appropriateness of finding meaning in the larger but essentially similar horror of Auschwitz and Treblinka by placing it in the context of a story of salvation. Some believers insist that it must still be right to do that. Others cannot conscientiously agree. To them, as to Ivan Karamazov, it seems wrong to find any meaning in the horrors except the evilness of evil and such bits of heroism and human decency as can be salvaged from the ruins. The horror, they think, needs more distance from God than traditional theologies of providence provide. Believers who are moved to respond to moral horrors in this way certainly have a motive to adopt a noninterventionist theory of divine action such as Maurice Wiles offers us.

Their position commands respect. I am not prepared to accept it, but I certainly would not pretend to refute it in a brief comment. I shall try, however, to make clear some of the costs that are likely to be incurred by a theodicy that refuses to locate horrors in a story of salvation.

Theodicies normally proceed by trying to relate evils to a proposed account of God's (actual or possible) activity and purposes. In Professor Wiles's noninterventionist free-will theodicy, the divine activity is understood exclusively as creating and sustaining a world of creatures that act by the powers God has given them, and the purpose on which God's permission of evil is seen as based is the purpose of enabling creatures to act freely. "Freely" is obviously used here in a sense incompatible with complete determinism. And the effective and meaningful freedom of creatures is seen as requiring both the background of a stable and predictable natural order, and a certain relinquishing by God of control over the creatures. Now Professor Wiles certainly has not said that this concern for freedom exhausts God's purposes for the world. Indeed, he has not implied that he is among those who would refuse to view horrors in the context of a story of salvation. But so far as I can see, the moral argument he has offered for a noninterventionist view of divine activity is based entirely on a free-will theodicy such as I have sketched, and on the question of what view of divine activity accords best with that theodicy. I shall therefore raise some questions about the adequacy of the free-will theodicy.

I return to Giovanni Pisano's faces of horror. The faces twisted in grief and pain, tortured, wild with anguish. But not only those; also the faces distorted by cruelty and guilt. Why would God permit this horror? What would be worth it? Free will? The free will of the killers? Is it a saving grace that they could have done otherwise? Or does that only add to the horror of guilt? Whatever nobility freedom may retain even in the abuse of it, few have thought a good God would permit great evils solely in order to make free sinning possible. The usual claim of a free-will theodicy is that the sins had also to be permitted in order that good deeds of creatures might be free. So consider good deeds, in particular the deeds (if we may call them that) of not murdering or torturing, and in general of refraining from great evils. Is it worth permitting the horrors of Auschwitz in order that the virtuous agent might truly say, "I refrained on my own, without too much help from God or other people"? Should we even wish to make that boast?

That is a very short objection to a free-will theodicy. Perhaps it is sentimental and ill considered—or perhaps not. But at least the following point is hard to reject. We could still have very extensive freedom even if we were unable, by nature or through frequent divine interventions, to perpetrate torture or genocide. Perhaps the freedom remaining to us would be somewhat less impressive than the freedom we actually have, but I think we should be very reluctant to claim that that difference, of itself, is worth the horrors that might have been prevented.

We have also to consider the phenomena that give great empirical plausibility to some forms of the doctrine of original sin. Even supposing our behavior is not totally determined causally, the occurrence of some significant moral evils is overwhelmingly probable in every human life. And by virtue of their formative experiences some individuals seem tragically likely to be involved in moral evils that will wreak real havoc on their lives and their possibilities for moral growth in this world. With these phenomena in mind it is natural to ask whether an omnipotent deity creating a world to be mainly a theater for the free development and exercise of virtue could not and would not have created the world somewhat differently in a way that would probably have led to more virtue and less vice. Of course we are not in a position to give a definitive answer to that question; but I think by far the most plausible answer is probably yes.

For reasons of these sorts I do not think it very plausible to suppose that an omnipotent and good deity has the possible free development and exercise of virtue by creatures as a sole purpose in creating and sustaining a world that contains the sorts of evils we know to exist. This is not to deny that the possibility of created freedom and its virtuous use is *among* the divine purposes to which a theodicist may wisely appeal. But this purpose needs to be connected with other purposes in a larger theological context. It is one of the advantages of a story of salvation to provide such a larger context. And if we are providing a larger context, it is in relation to that whole context, and not just to a theory of free will, that we must assess the appropriateness of an interventionist or noninterventionist view of God's activity. There are many directions one could go from this point. I shall simply suggest two features often found in theistic stories of salvation, and argue, first, that they are advantageous for theodicy, and, second, that they are supportive of somewhat interventionist accounts of divine activity in the world.

One of the most prominent features of stories of salvation in the major theistic traditions is life after death for human beings. This belief has played a large part in theodicies, and more broadly in accounts of God's purposes in relation to evils. Its most obvious function, of course, is not to explain the origin of evil, but to provide a context in which we can believe in a real triumph of good over evil, and a full experience of God's goodness and love to us—a triumph and a fullness such as most humans, at any rate, have not experienced, and seem quite unlikely to experience, in this life. If we have such a hope, it will certainly make a difference to our view of the problem of evil.

To this we may add that by offering a much larger theater for the working out of God's purposes for us, the belief in life after death opens the way for some accounts of God's purposes in permitting evils—accounts that would otherwise be impossible or most implausible. An important case in point is the idea of the world as a "vale of soul-making," of which John Hick has made such important use in his theodicy. "Soul-making" here signifies a development of human lives that is much more complex in its dimensions of value than the moral merit on which the unadorned free-will theodicy turns. To that extent it is more plausible to suppose that soul-making is worth the evils supposed to have been permitted for its sake than that mere moral merit is. But how far does soul-making get in this life? It seems to be broken off in a rather fragmentary condition at the deaths of many, perhaps most people. Often it is frustrated through circumstances largely beyond the individual's control, so far as this life is concerned. A soul-making theodicy is therefore not likely to work very well without a belief in life after death, which of course provides the context that Hick envisages for it.

For reasons such as these I think that a theologian who adopted a noninterventionist view of divine action at the price of giving up belief in life after death would probably be stepping out of the frying pan into the fire, as far as the problem of evil is concerned. Not that Professor Wiles's essay commits him inescapably to paying that price; it may be debated whether life after death necessarily involves a miracle in the sense in which he rejects miracles. Those theologians who have believed in the natural immortality of the soul have not regarded its survival after death as a miracle. And while the triumph of good in a life after death is normally envisaged as involving God's taking a direct hand in a lot of events there, it might be claimed that this takes place in a separate realm, outside the physical nature that we now inhabit, and is thus quite consistent with God's pursuing a strict noninterventionist policy in the world of our present experience.

To many of us, however, it will seem more plausible to regard life after death as miraculous rather than naturally inevitable, whether or not we think of it as involving literal physical resurrection of our bodies. A conception of bodily resurrection has traditionally been a part of Jewish and Christian belief in life after death, and is present in the New Testament. A case can be made, indeed, for saying that it is the central miracle for the New Testament. Some might object that that title belongs rather to the resurrection of Jesus; but I think the objection only proves the point. For the resurrection of Jesus is consistently regarded in the New Testament as the first fruits of the resurrection of all the dead.

This "first fruits" relation indicates another way in which an interventionist conception of divine activity in this world may be supported by a story of salvation that finds its culmination in a life beyond death. We would not find much satisfaction or plausibility in a story of salvation in which life on the other side of death was simply discontinuous with life on this side. Glimpses and foretastes of the future life may help to orient this life in hope to the coming triumph of good. And if that hope is for a direct and mighty action of God, may it not appropriately be sustained in this life by occasional miracles, as smaller, anticipatory direct actions of God? I take it that miracles are typically understood in this way in the New Testament, as "signs" of the Kingdom of God that is already present but not yet completely manifested or fulfilled.

What I am suggesting is that miracles, direct divine interventions in this world, make sense, and seem appropriate, against a background of more or less traditional eschatological belief, in a way that they do not if we suppose God's purposes for human life to be exhausted by the provision of a theater for possibly virtuous free action. Not that such provision for human freedom is necessarily excluded from a more eschatological view of God's purposes. On the contrary, what I envisage here is a system of divine purposes complex enough to incorporate some tensions. The orientation of human life toward God's future triumph provides a reason for anticipatory divine interventions, but the needs of a context for the exercise of human freedom provide a reason for having miracles only occasionally.

Having only occasional miracles gives rise to problems of fairness, as Wiles suggests. I am not suggesting a story of salvation whose full development would provide a complete solution to all such problems; that is probably impossible for human understanding. But I do think a background of eschatological belief may help us to see those problems as less than decisive. They may well seem decisive if we think the goods and evils to be distributed in this life are the only goods and evils that await us. But suppose we think "the sufferings of this present time are not worth comparing with the glory that is to be revealed to us" (Rom. 8:18 RSV)—not because the former are so slight but because the latter is so great. Then we may well welcome signs of the greater good breaking miraculously into the present life, even if that involves some inequity in the distribution of the lesser goods and evils.

I turn now to the second feature of many theistic stories of salvation that I promised to discuss, which is that salvation is sought, and seen as offered, in a personal relationship with God. God is not only Maker and Ruler, but also Friend, and even Lover. God's love for each one of us and our (actual or possible) love for God are regarded as central to the meaning of each human life.

This idea has more than one advantage for theodicy. To begin with, a personal relationship with God, in which one not only sees and loves God, but also is loved by God, is reasonably seen as the greatest good that can be offered to us, and its full development as at least a part of the glory to be revealed, with which the sufferings of the present time are not worthy to be compared. In the second place, a conception of life as lived in personal relationship with God provides a framework rich in meanings that are important in responding theologically to evils. It is in the context of such a relationship that it makes most sense to think of sins as forgiven, of hardships as occasions for trust in God, and of sufferings as shared with God.

Finally, the belief that personal relationship with us is one of God's aims in dealing with us seems to me important for the employment of the idea of free will in theodicy. My point is most easily grasped from the point of view of those who are sufficiently inclined to compatibilism to think that the best of human relationships, and the lives of the saints and moral heroes (the life of a Gandhi, for example) would still be quite wonderful even if causal determinism were true. From such a standpoint the question I raised earlier about the value of the relevant sort of freedom, the question whether God's exercising more control over the relevant human behavior would have been too high a price to pay for the elimination of the most horrible of the world's evils, will seem particularly urgent. And in answering it one may wish to draw on the belief that we are created for personal relationship with God.

Surely the complete determination of our behavior and attitudes by God would undermine the significance and value of our personal relationship with God much more clearly than it would undermine the worth of our relationships with other people. If our love for God were completely determined by God, and not just by forces or natures in some way independent of God, what would it be worth to God? Could our relationship with God in that case really be a friendship? John Hick compares this case with attitudes toward a hypnotist caused by the hypnotist himself through posthypnotic suggestion, commenting: "Just as the patient's trust in, and devotion to, the hypnotist would lack for the latter the value of a freely given trust and devotion, so our human worship and obedience to God would lack for Him the value of a freely offered worship and obedience [if God so controlled us as to *guarantee* those responses]. We should, in relation to God, be mere puppets, precluded from entering into any truly personal relationship with Him."[1] Thinkers of compatibilist

---

1. John Hick, *Evil and the God of Love*, revised edition (San Francisco: Harper and Row, 1978), 274. I have discussed this point at greater length in "Plantinga on the Problem of Evil,"

inclinations may grant this point even if they believe that complete determination of our behavior and attitudes by nature or by God would not
destroy the personal character of our relationships with each other, since
we would not ourselves be controlling each other thereby.

Incompatibilists may believe, of course, that determinism would undermine something of great value in human relationships and actions
even apart from considerations of personal relationship with God. But
even from an incompatibilist perspective, as I suggested earlier, we may
well question whether our free will is valuable *enough*, in the contexts in
question, to justify permitting the evils that have occurred. From this
standpoint too the theodicist may welcome the additional consideration
of the value that the freedom of creatures has for a personal relationship
with God.

There are several ways, then, in which belief in a personal relation
between us and God may be important for theodicy. And the belief is
clearly favorable to an interventionist view of God's action in the world;
God relates more personally to us in intervening to bring about some
result in our lives than in creating and sustaining the universe as a whole.
From our side, moreover, it is important to the personal character of our
relationship to God if we feel that we can pray to God for help in any
aspect of our lives. This sort of prayer does not require belief in *frequent
miracles*. But if it is to have the character I have in mind, it does require
a belief that God will at least consider responding with some direct action
in the world, and may in principle so act. Therefore, if it is a main part
of God's purposes for us to foster a personal relationship with us, God
has a reason to intervene *sometimes*, and perhaps to work miracles *occasionally*, even if divine purposes regarding our freedom require that
miracles should be infrequent.

This is a point at which the idea of a ruler or governor as an image for
God may have become theologically unhelpful. That image acquired its
leading, perhaps even dominant role in theology in societies in which it
typically signified a king who ruled personally, rather than as an agent of
an impersonal institution, and whose relationship with his subjects was
conceived as in some ways personal. Even Solomon, who ruled in splen-
dor over a mini-empire, is depicted as personally adjudicating a child-
custody dispute between two prostitutes (1 Kings 3:16–28). Our ideas of

in *Alvin Plantinga*, ed. James E. Tomberlin and Peter van Inwagen, in the *Profiles* series (D.
Reidel: Dordrecht, 1985), 227f.

good government are quite different. For all our bad-mouthing of bureaucracy, we are uncomfortable with governments whose style is personal rather than bureaucratic. We suspect them of corruption. Perhaps indeed our conceptions of justice require us to regard a personal style of government as *constituting* corruption.

If we apply our conceptions of good government to the image of God as governor, we may be tempted to infer that God's government must be bureaucratic rather than personal—though of course we are not likely to put it that way. This move would obviously be favorable to a noninterventionist view of God's activity in the world. But I think it is also a losing move for theology. It is not just that we dislike bureaucracy; for dislike is not, from a religious point of view, the most inadmissible attitude toward a deity. More important, we *despise* bureaucracy. We rely on bureaucracy, in some ways we demand it, but we also hold it in contempt. And contempt is the most inadmissible attitude toward a deity.

In this situation I think we would be well advised, not to eliminate governmental images for God and God's relation to us, but to limit their role in theology. Images of God as Parent, Lover, Friend, may be more important if we believe that we figure in the divine purposes as partners in a system of personal and social relationships with God, and not merely as parts of a system to which God is more impersonally and externally related. As I have indicated, I believe the more personalistic view has important resources to offer theodicy. And even apart from considerations of theodicy, I believe it is more in keeping with central concerns of Christianity.

I have left undiscussed some well-known objections—empirical, metaphysical, and religious—that have been raised against belief in life after death and in personal relationship with God, as well as against interventionist conceptions of divine action in the world. But I have supposed that I had quite enough to do in trying to deal with the moral issues raised in Professor Wiles's chapter.

CHAPTER 2

DIVINE ACTION: SHADOW OR SUBSTANCE?

William P. Alston

1

It is a truism that divine action is at the heart of the Christian tradition, and other theistic traditions. The Christian God is, preeminently, a God Who Acts. Nor is this action confined to such wholesale endeavors as the creation and conservation of the universe. God is portrayed as active in particular ways at particular times and places. He calls people, and peoples, to do His work. He aids them in specific ways in that work, for example, by putting words in their mouths and by confounding their enemies. He guides the deliberations and decisions of the church. Most dramatically, He works for the salvation of mankind and the reconciliation of mankind with Himself in the life, death, and resurrection of Jesus of Nazareth. More pervasively, He is in personal interaction with all who turn to Him, engaging in dialogue and other forms of personal interaction with them. Surely if one were to deny that God is active in the world in ways such as these, one would be distancing oneself in the most decisive way possible from the Christian tradition.

And yet the traditional understanding of divine action has been widely rejected in nonfundamentalist twentieth-century theology. When I speak of the "traditional understanding" I am not thinking of anything so completely specific and detailed as the theory of divine action one finds in a particular theologian. (Christian theologians differ on various points concerning the divine nature and at least some of these differences have an important bearing on what it is for God to act. For example, there is the question of whether God's own life is temporal or atemporal; the position on this issue will make a large difference in the construal of divine action.[1] Again, it is notorious that process theologians and more classical theologians construe divine action very differently.) Rather, I am referring to the very general conviction that when one speaks of God as giving me a task or enabling Jones to love others in a new way, one is *literally* attributing a particular intentional, purposive action to God, literally claiming that God has brought it about that a certain intention of His has been carried out. We are saying something that is true or false depending on whether God has indeed brought it about that the intended state of affairs was actualized. In short, according to this traditional understanding, if what we believe about divine actions is true, then God *really does* what we believe that He does!

It makes an important difference to our understanding of divine action just how we think of the concept thereof as related to the concept of human action. When I said that the "traditional understanding" was that God *literally* does what He is credited with doing, I did not mean to imply that action terms are applied *univocally* to God and human beings. Despite the common conflation of 'literal' and 'univocal' they are clearly distinct. For example, the terms 'force' and 'field' are used literally in physics, in the appropriate senses, but not univocally with their uses in common speech. And so it can be in theology. The question of just how talk of God's acting is related to talk of human beings' acting is a thorny one. There are obvious differences. God does not bring things about by moving His body, nor is His action dependent on causal processes within Him that are independent of His will. But it is not obvious that these

---

1. See, e.g., Nelson Pike, *God and Timelessness* (London: Routledge and Kegan Paul, 1970) and Eleonore Stump and Norman Kretzmann, "Eternity," *Journal of Philosophy* 78, no. 8 (August 1981), 429–58.

differences are reflected in differences in the *meaning* of action terms such as 'speak,' 'comfort,' 'condemn,' and 'forgive.' After all, it is a familiar phenomenon that one and the same term in one and the same meaning (e.g., 'animal') can be applied to widely different things.[2] I myself hold that although there are differences in meaning between, say, 'forgave' in 'God forgave me' and 'Sam forgave me,' there is a "univocal core" that is common to the two contexts, and that gives us a solid basis of intelligibility to the truth claim that God forgave me. In both cases we have the basic notion of an agent bringing something about in order to carry out an intention. And although 'intention' is not completely univocal in the divine and human case either, here too there is a partial univocity that provides a guaranteed intelligibility for the truth claims involved.[3] Obviously, my particular views on theological predication are not required for the traditional understanding. But I do believe that some significant carryover from concepts of human action to concepts of divine action is required for us to make full-blooded attributions of particular actions to God.

The traditional understanding attributes to God a large multiplicity of acts, differentiated by their involving different intentions to bring about different states of affairs at different times and places. This diversity is most obviously required by those actions that are divine responses to the actions of free creatures like us and divine responses to situations affected by our actions. Where only causally determined phenomena are involved, God could conceivably carry out His purposes just as well by a single intention to create and structure the natural order in a certain way. If it is God's purpose that the earth should form as a satellite of the sun during a certain period (and this is completely independent of the free choices of creatures), this could be taken care of in the original programming. But suppose, as I shall be supposing in this paper, that God has deliberately refrained from deciding what the free actions of created personal agents will be; He has endowed them with the capacity to decide certain things for themselves. Suppose also, as I shall, that God

2. See my "Can We Speak Literally of God?" in *Is God GOD?*, ed. A. D. Steuer and J. W. McClendon, Jr. (Nashville, Tenn.: Abingdon, 1981), reprinted in my *Divine Nature and Human Language* (Ithaca, N.Y.: Cornell University Press, 1989).

3. For the details, see my "Functionalism and Theological Language," *American Philosophical Quarterly* 22 (July 1985): 221–30, and "Divine and Human Action," in *Divine and Human Action*, ed. T. V. Morris (Ithaca, N.Y.: Cornell University Press, 1988), both reprinted in my *Divine Nature and Human Language*.

does not know prior to the creation what these choices will be.[4] In that case God's responses to those decisions, and to whatever is significantly influenced by them, cannot be part of His original creative intention. Since He does not know what those choices are until the agents are created and He can "see" what they do, He cannot choose His response as part of His original creative act. God must make each response "on the spot," forming a separate intention to deal with each. And, we should add, it is divine actions of this sort that are highlighted in the Christian tradition. It is God's interactions with us that are of the greatest religious interest, not His dealings with galaxies, planets, and interstellar spaces.

Thus on the traditional conception God carries out particular intentions at particular times and places in the history of the universe. Over and above His more fundamental role of being responsible for the existence and continued operation of all created things, He enters the process from time to time as an agent Who intentionally brings about particular states of affairs: that Jesus is alive after having been dead, that a certain message is communicated to Jones, and that Smith has more enthusiasm for her volunteer work. Furthermore, His agency is essential to these outcomes. They would not have happened, or would not have happened in just this way, if only created agents had influenced the outcome.

It need not be the case that God *directly* brings about everything He intends to bring about, though, being omnipotent, He could do so. According to the tradition, many intended outcomes are brought about through created agencies. He brings Israel to the promised land by inspiring and strengthening certain people to lead them there, not just by willing that they are there rather than in the desert. In guiding the church He works through the deliberations and debates of church people and councils. He brings people to His service by so arranging the circumstances of their lives that they are motivated to serve Him. Nevertheless, wherever divine agency is making a specific difference to the course of events, there will be something(s) that He brings about directly. In the

4. This does not have to be a temporal 'prior.' If God's being is timeless, then none of His cognitions, intentions, volitions, or actions are temporally before or after others. But there are other modes of priority and posteriority. A bit of knowledge can be said to be prior to God's creative act provided it is possible for God to take it into account in that act. And it can be argued that even if God is timeless, it is not possible for Him to take into account the nature of free creaturely actions in deciding the details of the creation.

Please note that I am not suggesting that these two suppositions are part of the "traditional understanding." On the contrary, one or both are rejected by many thinkers who share that understanding. They figure here as assumptions I am making for my discussion of the issues.

first example above it will be an altered state of mind and capacity of certain leaders. In the second case it will be the trains of thought of individuals within the church. And so on. The argument for this is just the argument for the general thesis in action theory that any nonbasic intentional action is supervenient on a basic intentional action, where a basic action is one that is done not *by* doing something else. I let you in by opening the door; I open the door by grasping the doorknob, turning it, and pulling the door; I grasp the doorknob by moving my hand in a certain way in a certain spatial relation to the knob. None of the first three actions mentioned are basic actions, for each is done by doing something else. But, on pain of an infinite regress, at some point we must reach an action that I *just do,* not by doing something else. It is plausible here to think that we reached that point with the fourth action specified, moving my hand in a certain way. It is plausible to suppose that there is nothing else I do in order to move my hand.[5] And so it is for the divine case. Whenever God does something by doing something else, there is at some point something He just does. This will not be a bodily movement, God having no body. It will be the voluntary bringing about of some effect in the created world.

It will be noted that I have thus far abstained from speaking of God's specific acts in the world as divine "interventions" or "interferences." Though this terminology may be, strictly speaking, accurate, in that I am thinking of God as providing a causal input that alters how things would have gone had only natural factors been operative, still it has the unfortunate implication that the normal procedure is the purely natural one and that divine action involves a departure from that norm. From the point of view of the Christian tradition, it is much better to think of the normal as God's usual way of dealing with His creation, which involves both purely natural causation, much of the time, and special divine causal inputs some of the time. One is no more untoward or "interfering" or "interventionist" than another. After all, this is God's creation. Talk of divine "intervention" stems from a deist picture of God as "outside" His creation, making quick forays or incursions from time to time and then re-

5. This supposition is controversial. Some would say that I move my hand by contracting certain muscles, and that I do that by sending certain neural signals from the brain. On this view, all basic actions are alterations of brain states. I myself think it implausible to suppose that people have intentions to affect brain states in specifiable ways. Hence I shall follow common practice and take our moving parts of the body that are ordinarily regarded as under direct voluntary control as being basic actions.

treating to His distant observation post. But despite these qualms, I shall frequently use the term "divine intervention," since I know of no comparably concise way of referring to the intentional divine production of a particular state of affairs at a particular place and time.

2

As indicated above, this traditional way of thinking of divine action has been widely abandoned in twentieth-century theology. The major factor in this shift has undoubtedly been the modern conviction that the universe exhibits a closed causal determinism, that every happening is uniquely determined to be just what it is by natural causes within the universe. (I shall refer to this thesis as "determinism," leaving 'causal' and 'natural' to be understood.) Determinism is obviously incompatible with the traditional conception. On the latter, God will sometimes bring about a state of affairs that would not have eventuated if only natural factors were involved; hence such happenings are not uniquely determined by purely natural causes. Here is a sampling of statements by twentieth-century theologians along this line.

> The traditional conception of miracle is irreconcilable with our modern understanding of both science and history. Science proceeds on the assumption that whatever events occur in the world can be accounted for in terms of other events that also belong within the world; and if on some occasions we are unable to give a complete account of some happening—and presumably all our accounts fall short of completeness—the scientific conviction is that further research will bring to light further factors in the situation, but factors that will turn out to be just as immanent and this-worldly as those already known.[6]

> . . . [C]ontemporary theology does not expect, nor does it speak of, wondrous divine events on the surface of natural and historical life. The causal nexus in space and time which Enlightenment

6. John Macquarrie, *Principles of Christian Theology*, 2d ed. (New York: Scribner's, 1977), 248.

science and philosophy introduced into the Western mind . . . is also assumed by modern theologians and scholars; since they participate in the modern world of science both intellectually and existentially, they can scarcely do anything else. Now this assumption of a causal order among phenomenal events, and therefore of the authority of the scientific interpretation of observable events, makes a great difference to the validity one assigns to biblical narratives and so to the way one understands their meaning. Suddenly a vast panoply of divine deeds and events recorded in Scripture are no longer regarded as having actually happened. . . . Whatever the Hebrews believed, we believe that the biblical people lived in the same causal continuum of space and time in which we live, and so one in which no divine wonders transpired and no divine voices were heard.[7]

Note that both of these statements appeal to "our modern understand-

7. Langdon B. Gilkey, "Cosmology, Ontology, and the Travail of Biblical Language," *Journal of Religion* 41 (1961), 194–205. Reprinted in *God's Activity in the World: The Contemporary Problem*, ed. Owen C. Thomas (Chico, Calif.: Scholars Press, 1983), 31. Note that Macquarrie gives a much more adequate formulation of what it is that comes into conflict with the traditional understanding. To affirm "the causal continuum of space and time" or "a causal order among phenomenal events" is simply to commit oneself to the less than startling proposition that there are causal interactions within the spatio-temporal universe, that some things do happen because of the operation of natural causes. But that is quite compatible with some events being, in whole or in part, the result of divine activity instead. To get something with more of a cutting edge we need something like the thesis of determinism, as formulated above, something that is clearly indicated in the passage from Macquarrie.

Some theologians go so far as to declare divine intervention to be *unintelligible or meaningless:*

> I want to emphasize that the problem we are considering does not arise in the first instance out of difficulties connected with conceiving a transcendental agent; it is rather the difficulty—even impossibility—of conceiving the finite event *itself* which is here supposed to be God's act. . . . An "event" without finite antecedents is no event at all and cannot be clearly conceived; "experience" with tears and breaks destroying its continuity and unity could not even be experienced . . . it is impossible to conceive such an act either as a natural event or as a historical event, as occurring either within nature or history; in short it is impossible to conceive it as any kind of event (in the finite order) at all. Our experience is of a unified and orderly world; in such a world acts of God (in the traditional sense) are not merely improbable or difficult to believe: they are literally inconceivable. It is not a question of whether talk about such acts is true or false; it is, in the literal sense, meaningless; one cannot make the concept hang together consistently. (Gordon Kaufman, "On the Meaning of 'Act of God,'" in *God the Problem* [Cambridge: Harvard University Press, 1972], 248)

To this I can only say that Kaufman has much too slight a regard for human powers of conception.

ing," "the assumption of a causal order among phenomenal events," and "the authority of the scientific interpretation of observable events." They simply point out that the traditional conception is incompatible with various things that are widely accepted today, things that claim "scientific authority." But this is hardly of probative value. Let us grant that the traditional conception runs counter to various features of the contemporary intellectual climate. But unless we have reason to think that our age is distinguished from all others in being free of intellectual fads and fancies, of attachments to assumptions that far outstrip the available evidence, of believing things because one finds one's associates believing them, then the mere fact that a view contradicts what is widely assumed today is of no particular significance to the epistemic evaluation of that view. What we need to consider is whether the reasons we have for these assumptions provide adequate support.

Why should we suppose that every happening in the universe is uniquely causally determined by factors within the universe? So far as I can see, the only respectable reason for determinism comes from reflection on the remarkable success of modern physical science in extending our knowledge of the natural conditions on which one or another outcome depends. On the one hand, it can be said that science assumes determinism; if scientists were not assuming that everything has natural causes, why would they devote so much time and energy to looking for them? On the other hand, it can be argued that the success science has enjoyed in this enterprise gives support to the thesis that there are always such conditions to be found. But a closer look reveals that these considerations fall far short of establishing determinism. As for the idea that science assumes determinism, the only thing a scientist is committed to assuming, by virtue of engaging in the scientific enterprise, is that there is a *good chance* that *the phenomena he is investigating* depend on natural causal conditions *to a significant degree*. These three qualifications mark three ways in which he need not be assuming strict determinism. He need only assume a significant probability, he need only make his assumption for the particular area of his investigation, and he need not assume even there (even a chance of) *complete* determination. As for the results of science, they are indeed impressive, but they fall far short of showing that every event in the universe is strictly determined to be just what it is by natural factors. All our evidence is equally compatible with the idea that natural causal determination is sometimes, or always, only approximate. We have observed only a tiny proportion of natural events.

Our observations are always subject to a margin of error; indeed, we exploit this fact to correct observations into a good fit with deterministic laws. In many cases we work with deterministic laws only at the price of construing the laws in terms of idealizations (frictionless surfaces, point masses, and the like) which actual occurrences only approximate. Thus the results of science might reasonably be taken to suggest a close approximation to natural determinism rather than the full-blown article.

Let me elaborate the point that particular divine actions would not jeopardize, or otherwise adversely affect, anything fundamental to science. Let's first confine ourselves to purely physical and biological phenomena, leaving the human psyche for a second stage. Let's say that God brings it about that Robinson recovers from a disease from which he would have died if nature had taken its course. Now, no doubt, medical researchers presuppose that pathological conditions are due to ascertainable natural causes, so that by discovering these we can put ourselves in a better position to forecast, prevent, and cure diseases. Does this require the assumption that every detail of every illness is rigidly determined by natural causes? Many medical scientists will, no doubt, assume this, but I cannot see that it is at all essential to their enterprise. Physicians are often surprised by recoveries as well as by relapses and by failures to improve. Every practicing physician can remember a number of cures that were miraculous so far as she can tell. To be sure, the fact that no one can specify the natural causal determinants of an event does not imply that it has none. Nevertheless, and this is the point I am concerned to make, the conduct of medical science is not at all affected by these inexplicable happenings. Even if they remain forever inexplicable in terms of natural causes, that will not slow down medical research. Medical research, like other scientific research, is concerned to establish generalizations that are close enough to being unqualifiedly true to be useful. So long as it is *generally* the case that the onset, development, and cure of pneumonia follows certain natural regularities, that will give the scientist all he needs; a few exceptions do not matter. Whether or not God ever intervenes, scientists not infrequently run into particular cases they cannot understand and which do not fit the best generalizations they can formulate. They, quite properly, ignore these in the search for principles that fit the overwhelming majority of the cases.

As for the psychological and sociological, our scientific achievements cannot begin to match those in the physical and biological realms. It would be flying in the face of fact to suggest that the development of these disciplines support the idea that psychological and social phenomena are rigidly determined. Many people assume this, but if they have any reasons for the assumption they stem from general philosophical considerations rather than from scientific advances. Thus the claim that God directly produces in Hailey a greater interest in spiritual matters or a greater resistance to drug addiction can hardly be thought to conflict with anything the social and psychological sciences have given us reason to accept. And as for the necessity of assuming determinism here in order to conduct research, the considerations of the last two paragraphs apply here as well.

Let me say something about the common idea that the traditional conception of divine activity involves "violating" laws of nature. That conception, as we have seen, does involve thinking of God as bringing things about other than they would have been had only natural factors been operative. But whether that implies a "violation" of natural laws depends on how we think of the latter. To suppose that it does is to presuppose that natural laws specify *unqualifiedly* sufficient conditions. Thus a law of hydrostatics might specify as an unqualifiedly sufficient condition for a body sinking in still water (of sufficient depth) that the body be of a density greater than the water. A man standing upright in the middle of a deep lake without sinking would be a violation of that law. But we are never justified in accepting laws like this. The most we are ever justified in accepting is a law that specifies what will be the outcome of certain conditions *in the absence of any relevant factors other than those specified in the law.* The laws we have reason to accept lay down sufficient conditions only within a "closed system," that is, a system closed to influences other than those specified in the law. None of our laws take account of all possible influences. Even if a formulation took account of all influences with which we are acquainted, we can never be assured that no hitherto unknown influences are lurking on the horizon. A man standing upright on the surface of a lake will sink, *unless* he is being supported by a device dangling from a helicopter, or *unless* he is being drawn by a motorboat, or *unless* a sufficiently strong magnetic attraction is keeping him afloat, and so forth. Since the laws we have reason to accept make provision for interference by outside forces unanticipated by the law, it can hardly be claimed that such a law will be violated if a divine outside force intervenes; hence it can hardly be claimed that such laws imply that God does not intervene, much less imply that this is impossible. No doubt that is not the sort of outside force scientists normally envisage, but that is neither here nor there. If we were to make the rider read "in the absence of outside forces of the sort we are prepared to recognize as such," our confidence in all our law formulations would be greatly weakened; we have no basis for supposing that science has at this point identified all the factors that can influence natural phenomena.

The upshot of all this is that, despite the enormous press given the thesis of determinism, I feel that it is not really a serious threat to the traditional way of thinking of God's actions in the world. But even if we cannot rule out the real possibility of divine interventions, there are well-known epistemological objections to claims to spot particular cases. And if we can never tell when and where God is active, the general category will be of little use to us. The classical formulation of these objections is found in David Hume's celebrated chapter on miracles in the *Enquiry Concerning Human Understanding*. Briefly put, the argument is that in order for something to count as a miracle (divine intervention), it must be contrary to the usual course of nature, contrary to the way things go when only natural causes are involved. But then there is a very strong inductive argument from experience against its occurrence. Hence we will be justified in accepting a report of such an occurrence only if our reasons for supposing the report to be veridical are even stronger than our reasons for the proposition that such things never happen; and this is never the case.

This argument poses a number of issues that I cannot pursue here. I shall confine myself to two points. First, it is not generally the case that alleged divine interventions go contrary to our experience. Especially in the case of divine grace, the changes allegedly wrought by the direct action of God do not run counter to any regularities established by our experience. Indeed, we have no significant inductive evidence for general laws governing a growth in sanctity or devotion to Christ. Hume's position seems plausible only when restricted to "physical" miracles, where there is a widely recognized "ordinary course of nature." Second, and this is a point that has often been made in the literature, the likelihood of a report of a miracle is profoundly influenced by one's background religious and metaphysical assumptions. If these include the principle that the world is created and governed by a being who has reasons to intervene from time to time, this will materially increase the probability of some such reports being correct, though it does not, of course, establish the correctness of any particular report. In any event, it is not my concern in this essay to determine how we should go about

identifying divine interventions. I am concerned only to argue for the
viability of the concept.

3

There are also theological objections to divine intervention, and, as will
appear, I find at least one of them to have more force than anything yet
considered, though I take them to fall far short of a conclusive case.

First, I shall consider a radical line of thought designed to show that
God is not an agent in any literal sense at all, and hence not an agent of
particular doings in the world. This contention goes back at least to
Friedrich Schleiermacher, who held that to think of God as a cause of
particular events is to reduce God to the status of a creature. It is to think
of God as a reality existing alongside other realities, operating in the
same field of causal influences as they. It is to "finitize" God, to reduce
Him to a finite being, even if the greatest one.[8] In this century contentions
like these are especially associated with the name of Paul Tillich.

> The being of God is being-itself. The being of God cannot be
> understood as the existence of a being alongside others or above
> others. If God is a being, he is subject to the categories of fini-
> tude, especially to space and substance. Even if he is called the
> "highest being" in the sense of the "most perfect" and the "most
> powerful" being, this situation is not changed. When applied to
> God, superlatives become diminutives. They place him on the
> level of other beings while elevating him above all of them. . . .
> Whenever infinite or unconditional power and meaning are attrib-
> uted to the highest being, it has ceased to be a being and has
> become being-itself.[9]

> . . . [G]rave difficulties attend the attempt to speak of God as

8. See *The Christian Faith*, trans. H. R. Mackintosh and J. S. Stewart (Edinburgh: T. and
T. Clark, 1928), 173, 179, 182. The last two references come from a section entitled, "It can
never be necessary in the interest of religion so to interpret a fact that its dependence on God
absolutely excludes its being conditioned by the system of Nature."

9. *Systematic Theology* (Chicago: University of Chicago Press, 1951), 1:235.

existing. . . . [T]he question of the existence of God can be neither asked nor answered. If asked, it is a question about that
which by its very nature is above existence, and therefore the
answer—whether negative or affirmative—implicitly denies the
nature of God. It is as atheistic to affirm the existence of God as
it is to deny it. God is being-itself, not a being.[10]

In a brief treatment I can hardly go into the rich texture of thought that
underlies these claims in Schleiermacher and Tillich. I shall have to
confine myself to the suggestion that thinking of God as bringing about
particular effects at particular times and places does not have the theologically aversive consequences these thinkers suggest. Why suppose
that if God sometimes directly brings about natural happenings, he is
therefore reduced to the status of a "finite creature"? Why must any
agent who contributes to some spatio-temporal occurrence be *finite*, much
less a *creature?* What is there to prevent an infinite creator from making
such a contribution? Is it that by entering the field "along with" natural
causes, God becomes "just another" reality or being "alongside" the latter? But, leaving aside the spatial metaphor of "alongside," God is certainly not "just another" being, however much He may directly bring
about in the world. Surely an omnipotent, omniscient perfectly good creator of all other than Himself is not "just another" being; He is a very
special being indeed. And how does it derogate from God's status to be
a being? What else is there to be? These theologians seem to think that
if God shares any activity, status, or category with creatures, that pulls
Him down to their level. That is a way of denying any univocal predication of God and creature, however attenuated. But these scare tactics
will not establish that position. In what respects does bringing about
particular effects in the world reduce God to the level of creatures? It
will certainly imply that both He and creatures are engaged in bringing
about states of affairs; that is, they are both agents. But it is a mere
rhetorical flourish to say that this puts Him on our level. Obviously there
is a world of difference, all the difference there can be, between an infi-
nite-source-of-all-being bringing about X, and you or me bringing about
X. The fact that we are both engaged in *bringing about something* should
not panic us into denying the differences between creator and creature
that the Christian tradition has insisted on. In short, I see no merit what-

10. *Systematic Theology,* 1:236–37.

soever in these allegations. Unless there is something more to be said on the matter than is made explicit by Schleiermacher, Tillich, and like-minded thinkers, I think that we can safely ignore the idea that being an agent that brings about particular effects in the world is incompatible with divine status.

From this point on I shall be referring to points made by Maurice Wiles in his 1986 Bampton Lectures.[11] One of the theological qualms expressed by Wiles concerns human free will, which he understandably and, I believe, justifiably, takes care to safeguard. If the attachment to divine intervention carries with it the picture of God as "absolute controller," the determiner of every detail of His creation, then this leaves no room for human freedom of choice (60, 81). And he seems to think that this unwanted entailment is inescapable. However, his actual argument is much narrower in scope. Thus he argues that God could not work through unwitting human agents, with no idea of their divinely appointed role, such as Cyrus, unless "there were some hidden manipulation of Cyrus' deliberative processes" (62). And as for the traditional idea of the gospel events as the fulfillment of prophecy, he holds that "the sort of fulfillment of prediction implied by the scriptural texts cited seems inconceivable apart from a manipulative control of human action that is wholly unacceptable" (63). But he makes no real attempt to mount this argument across the board. This abstention is certainly well advised. Purely physical and biological miracles—the plagues visited on Egypt, the parting of the waters of the Sea of Reeds, Jesus' healings and walking on the water, the resurrection—do nothing to violate anyone's freedom of choice, unless it is the choice to sink into the lake or to stay dead! Moreover, the operation of grace need not violate human freedom, though it has often been so construed. If divine grace involves the bringing about of such effects as the strengthening of some tendencies and the weakening of others, the greater salience of certain ideas and beliefs, a greater attractiveness of certain goals and a lesser attractiveness of others, then our free choice is left unimpaired, *so long as we do not think of these tendencies, ideas, and attractions as causally determining our decisions and actions.* And there is no need to do so. Human beings often perform actions specifically designed to influence the actions of others without violating their freedom. Why could not God do the same? No doubt God, unlike you, could override my freedom by issuing a divine fiat if He so chose;

11. *God's Action in the World* (London: SCM, 1986).

but He could make the opposite choice as well. For that matter, God could inspire Cyrus to free the Israelites from their Babylonian captivity without *determining* him to do so and leaving him no choice. He could simply make the prospect sufficiently attractive. (Even if you make me "an offer I cannot refuse," that does not imply that I do not freely choose to accept the offer.) Thus Wiles is far from having shown that there can be no divine interventions without loss of human freedom; nor do I see how this could be shown.

Wiles also emphasizes the following difficulty. If direct divine interventions do occur and hence are not incompatible with divine purposes, why are they distributed as they are? In particular, why does not God intervene to prevent the grossest of evils?

> Miracles must by definition be relatively infrequent or else the whole idea of laws of nature, even of a broadly statistical sort, would be undermined, and ordered life as we know it an impossibility. Yet even so it would seem strange that no miraculous intervention prevented Auschwitz or Hiroshima, while the purposes apparently forwarded by some of the miracles acclaimed in traditional Christian faith seem trivial by comparison. Thus to acknowledge even the possibility of miracle raises acute problems for theodicy. (66)

Moreover, if particular exercises of divine grace are carried out for some people and not others, or carried out more forcefully for some people than for others, how can God be acquitted of willful partiality?

> If we speak of God's call having 'peculiar force or specific efficacy' in some cases, that logically implies a lesser degree of force and efficacy in others. The apparent arbitrariness in a divine will that operates in such a way remains, and remains a serious objection to accepting such a picture. (79)

This is one argument I am not prepared to dismiss as lacking in force. It is a serious difficulty. In fact it is a particular form of the most serious of all difficulties for any form of theism: the problem of evil. But that fact alone suffices to reduce its force as an objection to divine intervention in particular. The point is that the problem of evil is so severe anyway, even if there is no divine intervention, that the accretion due to the distribution of divine intervention is hardly significant. Even if God's activity vis-à-vis creation is confined to initially setting things up in the way He does, there are more than enough questions as to why he has done it this way. Why did He not endow us with less painful signals of something amiss with the organism? Why did He not give us natures such that we are more strongly motivated to do things that are in our own long-range interest? Why did He leave us so vulnerable to natural disasters and disease? Why does He not make His existence and purposes more apparent? And so on. Christian thinkers have struggled to give answers to such questions, but none have carried general conviction. The appeal to the value of creaturely free will, emphasized by Wiles and countless others, contributes to answering the question of why there is human wrongdoing, but, except for highly questionable theories of the consequences of the Fall, it does nothing to answer questions like the above. Thus, quite apart from problems concerning divine intervention, we are faced with unanswered questions, perhaps unanswerable by us in this life, questions as to why God has devised His creation as He has. Hence, *if* a theistic position is tenable at all, it is tenable in the face of an inability to answer such questions, and so our inability to answer such questions concerning divine intervention can hardly be a conclusive reason for rejecting it. If our inability to answer such questions is a conclusive negative reason, then theism goes down the drain whether we accept divine intervention or not. And if it is not a conclusive negative reason, it leaves the belief in divine intervention standing.

4

Thus contrary to the strong current consensus, I do not believe that there are sufficient reasons to abandon the traditional view of divine action. It is a further question what basis we have for accepting it. I take it that for the Christian the main basis is to be found in the biblical record, the Christian tradition, and Christian experience. These sources support the view so strongly that I think it fair to say that Christians abandon it only under pressure from what they take to be sufficient contrary considerations. If I am right in supposing that the latter are far from adequate, that amounts to a defense of the view from within the Christian community.

Not everyone, even within that community, will be convinced by my defense. Hence it will not be amiss to take a look at what substitutes have been proposed by those who reject the traditional view. I cannot survey them all here. Continuing with Professor Wiles's Bampton Lectures, I shall focus attention on the one he develops there.[12] Here is the basic idea:

> . . . [T]he proposal that I want to make is that the primary usage for the idea of divine action should be in relation to the world as a whole rather than to particular occurrences within it. (28)

> . . . [T]he whole process of the bringing into being of the world, which is still going on, needs to be seen as one action of God. (29)

> . . . [W]e should see the gradual emergence of our world as a single divine act. In other words it is a purposeful occurrence, whose disparate features are held together by a unity of intention. (54)

> I had argued in earlier chapters that we can make best sense of this whole complex of experience and of ideas if we think of the whole continuing creation of the world as God's one act, an act in which he allows radical freedom to his human creation. The nature of such a creation, I have suggested, is incompatible with the assertion of further particular divinely initiated acts within the developing history of the world. God's act, like many human acts, is complex. I have argued that particular parts of it can rightly be spoken of as specially significant aspects of the divine activity, but not as specific identifiable acts of God. (93)

Thus God's one and only act vis-à-vis the world is His bringing it into existence. Before we examine what Wiles has to say about putative smaller divine acts, in the light of this proposal, we need to get clearer about the proposal.

First, it could be read as a merely verbal proposal to speak of alleged specific acts of God in history and in the lives of human beings as "aspects" of the one divine act rather than as different complete acts. This would make the issue one of how to individuate acts, a notorious problem

---

12. He acknowledges a predecessor in Kaufman, "On the Meaning of 'Act of God.'"

in action theory.[13] I shall take it that Wiles does not mean merely to be recommending a general mode of act individuation on which whatever God does counts as one act, but rather intends to be making a more substantive theological claim, one that implies not just that particular divine interventions are best thought of as components of a single act, but that they do not occur at all.[14]

Second, let us note that if God determines every detail of His creation, then He could bring about all the particular effects attributed to Him in the traditional view just by setting up the system initially in a certain way. That would enable us to hold that God's agency is responsible for "miracles," historical movements, impacts on the lives of particular persons, and everything else traditionally attributed to Him, while at the same time denying that He does anything vis-à-vis the creation over and above His bringing it into existence. The price of this would be not only an acceptance of complete determinism but also the inability to treat some events and not others as acts of God. On this view God would have knowingly determined everything by setting up the universe as He did. In any event, this is not what Wiles is up to, since he makes an unequivocal commitment to human free will in a "libertarian" sense in which it is incompatible with determinism.

So just how, on Wiles's view, is God's one act of creation (and, perhaps, sustenance)[15] related to the various events that are traditionally taken to be brought about by particular acts of God? A hard-nosed interpretation would run as follows. God is responsible for the existence of the universe, including human beings who have been so created by God as to enjoy a "radical degree of freedom" (26).[16] In doing so God has voluntarily subjected Himself to the risks inherent in giving creatures a

13. For example: if I *kill you* by *shooting you* by *firing a gun* by *pulling the trigger* by *moving my finger*, have I performed five different acts, or are these merely five aspects of a single act? Both answers have been defended. Again, into how many component acts are we to divide a complex sequential activity like building a bookcase?

14. To be sure, there are specific theological reasons for collapsing all divine acts into one, e.g., the doctrine of divine simplicity. The doctrine of divine timelessness might also be deployed for this purpose. However this would not seem to be Wiles's agenda.

15. It is not clear from his book whether Wiles wishes to distinguish creation and preservation (sustenance). Perhaps he thinks of "preservation" as "continuous creation," and holds that the latter is the only kind of creation there is. (On this point see Philip L. Quinn, "Divine Conservation, Continuous Creation, and Human Action," in *The Existence and Nature of God*, ed. Alfred J. Freddoso [Notre Dame, Ind.: University of Notre Dame Press, 1983]). This particular issue has no significant bearing on the points under discussion here.

16. See Wiles, *God's Action in the World*, chapters 2 and 3, on this point.

significant degree of freedom to make choices and carry them out, and thereby to affect others in various ways. Thus we must distinguish God's relation to the free and the unfree portions of His creation. As for the latter He has instituted a causal order and thereby determined how things go, *except for the extent to which it is affected by the free actions of creature.* As for the former, it is part of God's basic purpose in bringing free creatures into existence to let the chips fall where they may, even where they fall in ways that run counter to His purposes. His purpose of giving free creatures their autonomy takes precedence over any other purposes. This, of course, allows for God's having influenced free creaturely decisions by having endowed them with certain natures rather than others.[17] To sum up, as far as states of affairs and processes in the universe are free of the influence of creaturely freedom, there is no need for any special acts of God; that was all taken care of in the creation (97). As far as concerns free creaturely actions and what is affected by them, there is, so to say, "room" for specific divine responses, but His respect for the autonomy of free creatures inhibits Him from making them. Thus, and this is why I called this a "hard-nosed" interpretation, there is no place in the divine plan for any activity in the world other than the primal determination of the natures of creatures and their interrelations.

If this is the picture, then what do we say about what has persistently seemed to Christian experience to be specific responses of God to particular situations? Wiles's most substantive suggestion is that the interpretation of events like the conversion of Paul or Augustine as brought about by divine providence are "necessarily retrospective in character. They are examples of the fundamental human process of the search for meaning" (81). He continues:

> Why then the language of God's action at all? Because our lives are a part of God's personal act in the bringing into existence of the world, a world which includes as a paramount part of its purpose the self-dedication of human lives such as those of a Paul or an Augustine. It is precisely in them that God's act finds part of its fulfillment, not because there are separate distinguishable

17. Wiles quotes John Lucas as writing concerning Hitler's "providential" holding back of his panzers at the time of Dunkirk: "God's influence is to be seen not in an arbitrary interference with Hitler's free-will, but in having made men as he has made them, with the grain of human nature such that God's purposes tend to be fulfilled, and that those who would frustrate them are frustrated" (Wiles, *God's Action in the World*, 62).

divine initiatives in relation to them or to particular aspects of them but because the emergence of such lives is what God's one act deliberately seeks to make possible.

It is not clear to me exactly what role *retrospection* plays here, but the general thrust is clear enough. God's act of creation was carried out in the pursuit of certain purposes (e.g., the development of human beings into "sons of God");[18] that is, He set the universe up in this way to make it *possible* for these purposes to be fulfilled. When something happens that can be seen to further these purposes, it is attributed to God *as a way of expressing its relation to those purposes*. This is not to be read, then, as a claim that God was literally bringing about this occurrence by a separate act, but as a more vivid and pictorial way of acknowledging the event as a fulfillment of divine purpose.[19]

I cannot see that this understanding of providence and grace takes adequate account of the deliverances of Christian experience. I am not just saying that Wiles's position does not admit of specific divine responses to specific situations and hence is sharply at variance with the Christian tradition. That is obvious and is insisted on by Wiles himself. My point is, rather, that the pervasive sense, in the Christian community (and elsewhere), that we genuinely interact with God in various ways (and hence that God is a party to such interactions and so is engaged in intentional behavior toward us), is ruled out of court by this revisionary interpretation. I cannot see that any view that denies that God is carrying out specific intentions in His dealings with us can lay claim to support by the main weight of Christian experience. This is not the sort of claim that itself admits of conclusive support, for the question of how to formulate the content of the experience in question parallels the differences between theories of divine action. Let me just say this. From the beginning of the Judeo-Christian tradition, practically all those most articulate in speaking from their experience of God have felt impelled (presumably irresistibly) to report their experience in terms of God's doing things vis-à-vis them then and there. This would seem to create a considerable

18. This is my language, not Wiles's.

19. I have made a similar suggestion (as a possibility), developing some hints from Tillich and Macquarrie, in "God's Action in the World," *Evolution and Creation*, ed. Ernan McMullin (Notre Dame, Ind.: University of Notre Dame Press, 1986), reprinted in *Divine Nature and Human Language*. The pages in the latter are 217–21. The section is entitled "Special Acts of God without Direct Intervention."

burden of proof on anyone who would seek to depart from this consensus. Unless there are very strong reasons for denying such divine activity we should take it that the situation is as it seems experientially to be.[20] But I am convinced, by considerations of the sort sketchily surveyed in this essay, that there are no such reasons. Hence I can see no sufficient basis for abandoning the tradition in favor of a pale substitute of the sort offered by Wiles and other twentieth-century theologians.

5

I must confess that I may have presented Wiles's position as starker than he intended it. On the reading just given he portrays God as creating the universe with free creatures and, as far as they are concerned, taking His lumps, putting up with whatever results from their exercise of their freedom, however it goes. However, there is a question as to how this is related to the view that the ultimate fulfillment of God's purposes is assured. At one point Wiles writes:

> I have argued earlier that the strong sense of human freedom and creativity which process theology is determined to maintain can be affirmed within a theology that continues to affirm the absoluteness of God's creative work. May it perhaps also be compatible with a continued insistence that the intention of that creative work will not finally be thwarted? The religious sense of God as final succour believes that it is. It does not deny the risk inherent in creation. But it sees it as a risk of disasters on the road (a risk that would appear to have been abundantly realized) rather than a risk of ultimate failure. (50–51)

If this position is to avoid requiring God to make particular responses to particular situations in order to ensure the ultimate fulfillment of His purposes (the cosmic chessmaster), then it will presumably require that God have set limits to human freedom of such a sort as to ensure this. This is the idea expressed in the passage I noted earlier as quoted by

20. I assume that Wiles would agree with me on this and would only dissent from the next sentence.

Wiles from Lucas, in which the latter speaks of God as having made "human nature such that God's purposes tend to be fulfilled, and that those who would frustrate them are frustrated." Thus the thesis that God's purposes cannot ultimately be frustrated *can* be combined with the denial of any "on the spot" response of God to situations as they develop.

However, remember that Wiles in passages quoted above repeatedly speaks of God's one act of creation as "continuing" and as "still going on." Again he writes, "God's fundamental act, the intentional fruit of the divine initiative, is the bringing into existence of the world. That is a continuous process, and every part of it is therefore in the broadest sense an expression of divine activity" (107–8). Given Wiles's emphasis on creaturely freedom, how does he think of this one act of God as stretching over the entire cosmic process without involving specific reactions to specific situations? Is it just a matter of conserving and, so to say, reaffirming the basic natures of all creatures at each moment? Or is something more specific involved; and if so, how can that be squared with Wiles's denial of "on the spot" responses? The following passage seems to be saying that something more is involved.

> So God's will for the world can properly be spoken of not only in the generalized form that characterizes his one fundamental act of creation; it can also be spoken of in more precise and changing ways that take account of how the world now is as a result both of human achievements and of human sin. (104)

But, given the radical freedom that Wiles takes us to enjoy, how can God's activity "take account of how the world now is as result of human achievements and of human sin," without God's devising fresh responses to such situations as they develop? It certainly looks as if this is a point at which we can see a tension between Wiles's aversion to divine intervention and his recognition of God's concern for the ever-changing face of human activity and its consequences.

To sum up, since the traditional understanding of divine action is so massively supported by Scripture, tradition, and experience, it would take very strong reasons to dislodge it. I find no such reasons. And proposed substitutes do not look promising.

ALTERNATIVE CONCEPTIONS OF GOD

James M. Gustafson

William Alston defends the general view that God is to be interpreted as agent or actor, and he develops a particular interpretation of that idea. The bulk of his essay is a critical analysis of theologians who amend or reject that idea. My response is directed toward the backing for his constructive thesis; it is not a full defense of the positions he criticizes. But it is a response to his thesis in light of some of the theological concerns of the materials criticized and some of the biblical, traditional, and experiential backings that can be adduced for those concerns.

I begin my response by quoting from the very end of Alston's chapter. "To sum up, since the traditional understanding of divine action is so massively supported by Scripture, tradition, and experience, it would take strong reasons to dislodge it." Alston does not adequately provide evidences and arguments for the massive support for his thesis from those three sources. My response suggests all too briefly various contrary, if not contradictory, evidences from Scripture, tradition, and experience that need to be accounted for to support his summary statement. At the end of my response I indicate what some authors who use act and agency language see to be its ethical implications, and compare those with implications drawn from a different emphasis in the interpretation of God and God's relations to the creation, including nature and human activity. The first two sentences of the chapter provide the direction for my basic line of inquiry. "It is a truism that divine action is at the heart of the Christian tradition. The Christian God is, preeminently, a God Who Acts." What is included and excluded by the metaphor of the "heart?" What is included and excluded by "preeminently?"

1

Alston's argument depends upon biblical exegetical backing. I do not fault the essay for not providing full biblical support, since that would require a much more extensive account than is appropriate for its purpose. Since it assumes such support, however, it is fair to ask what Alston would do with biblical evidences that can be adduced for other ways of interpreting God and God's relation to the cosmos, our world, and human life. Certain of the Psalms focus attention on the power and glory of God seen through the beauties and the terrors of nature; I have in mind Psalms 19, 29, 93, 96, and particularly 104. We have what Jon Levinson calls "the frigid theocentrism" of Job 38:1–42:6. Other aspects of the Wisdom literature as found in Ecclesiastes and Proverbs, and particularly in the Apocrypha, can be cited as evidences of an understanding of God and God's relations to the creation and human life that is not centered on action so much as on power and order. It is not only humans that are to praise the Lord; the whole of creation does so, as in the passage in "The Song of the Three," which anticipates the famous prayer of St. Francis. The things that are to bless the Lord include the heavens, the waters above the heavens, the sun and moon, the stars, the rain and dew, the winds that blow, scorching blast and bitter cold, fire and heat, rime and snow, mountains and hills, and on and on. One thinks of Solomon's prayer at the dedication of the temple, 2 Chronicles 6:19ff., "But can God indeed dwell with man on earth? Heaven itself, the highest heaven cannot contain thee." It is at least arguable that in these and other places God is interpreted power and order, related to the world less as actor than as impersonal reality to be confronted and to be praised.

Does Alston's concept of divine action hold for all of the various metaphors and images of God and God's relations to nature and human life that one finds in the Bible? Or does it need much more specification and elaboration than he suggests? A random list of images will suffice to indicate what I think is worthy of discussion: God is creator, commander, lawgiver, speaker, king and sovereign, avenger and warrior, redeemer and savior, father, spirit, liberator. All of these are action terms, but they are very different from each other. The divine actions in the Bible have specific ends relative to the events and persons addressed or acted upon: some are historic and political events, others focus more on individuals as accountable persons. Alston clearly states that the theme of God as actor needs elaboration and specification. My point is to ask whether the variety of terms and metaphors used in the Bible, even those that are act-oriented, can be easily generalized, and whether the specification of kinds of action would alter his own more precise interpretation of the theme?

The language of the God Who Acts came to thematic prominence in theology in the middle of this century in a way it had not in many previous periods. It emerged in the context of a kind of biblical theology developed by nonfundamentalist Protestants. On the American scene, George Ernest Wright's *God Who Acts* was a summary and epitome of the view. One interpretation of why it emerged is that Protestant theology freed itself from the problems of what Kant called "physico-theology" by turning more to God's action in history. Canaanite religion was "nature" religion, biblical religion was history-oriented. In contrast to the "pagan gods," "in the Bible . . . God is known and addressed primarily in the terms which relate him to society and history. The language of nature is distinctly secondary."[1] This distinction between history and nature as the realm of divine presence was used widely—for example, in Gustavo Gutierrez's *A Theology of Liberation*, the Exodus narrative is one of the principal paradigms of God's action. He writes, "Other religions think in terms of cosmos and nature. Christianity, rooted in biblical sources, thinks in terms of history."[2] The adequacy of this generalization from the Bible certainly is being tested by other biblical scholars.

1. G. Ernest Wright, *God Who Acts: Biblical Theology as Recital* (London: SCM, 1952), 49.
2. Gustavo Gutierrez, *A Theology of Liberation* (Maryknoll, N.Y.: Orbis Books, 1973), 49.

With reference, then, to the biblical backing for Alston's claim, my query is whether the focus on the God Who Acts excessively subordinates other strands of the theology found in the Bible. If these other strands are not dominant, does that warrant their virtual elimination? And second, what nuancing or modification of the theme of the God Who Acts is required if we take into account the wide range of images of God's relation to the cosmos, to history, and to human life that can be found in the Bible?

2

A historical claim is made when Alston writes that "divine action is at the heart of the Christian tradition." One can inquire about evidences that sustain his view of the tradition, and about modifications of his judgment that might come from acknowledging other tendencies within it. One can ask about other terms, in contrast to "act," in the theological tradition. Alston seems to propose something general enough to include both Aquinas and Barth; this leads one to ask why Barth took such pains to define his views over against *analogia entis*. Barth, for example, wrote that "the fundamental Roman Catholic conception of the harmony, rooted in the concept of being, between nature and supernature, nature and grace, reason and revelation, man and God" made metaphysics "a basic discipline superior to both philosopher and theology."[3] Does Alston ignore the "being" tradition in Catholic theology? The polarity of act and being certainly has been used heuristically to elucidate significant differences in understanding God's relation to all that is, and constructively to argue for the correctness, or at least preferability, of one term over the other (for one twentieth-century discussion, see Bonhoeffer, *Act and Being*). In other of Alston's writings that I have not read, he may have addressed whether, in the theological tradition of both Eastern and Western Christianity, the language of act has primacy over the language of being.

Various evidences could be adduced from the theological tradition that would at least qualify Alston's generalization. My view is that the language of being, in quite impersonal terms, often exists side by side with

3. Karl Barth, *Ethics* (New York: Seabury, 1981), 31. See also *Church Dogmatics*, II / 2 (Edinburgh: T. and T. Clark, 1948), 530.

the language of act; Calvin would be one author in which both are found, though the language of being is not developed in the philosophic terms that others use. Furthermore, a range of terms can be found in the tradition that contrast with act language, or at least qualify its application; for example, the natural law participates in the *mind* of God, God's purposes are manifest in the *order* of creation and in the law by which God governs, etc.

What, from Alston's perspective, is the status of theological language that does not make act central? The tradition is more pluriform and complex than Alston suggests, and that fact provides backing for theologians who draw upon language that is not act-centered to develop systematic positions different from his.

3

Christian experience is the third main basis for support of Alston's general position. His discussion does not develop very specifically what range of experiences supports his view. The illustrations tend to focus on individual personal relations to God, which nicely cohere with the preference for act language. "It is God's interactions with us that are of the greatest religious interest, not His dealings with galaxies, planets, and interstellar spaces" (page 44). All of us who invoke experience as backing for our theological arguments are forced to make judgments about which experiences count as evidence for the claims we want to make about God's relations to all things. Alston does not clearly define in his essay what counts as Christian experience. What experiences that others might wish to adduce does his view exclude and why? The sentence I quoted above, for example, seems to rule out God's relations to the vastness of the cosmos as being of little religious "interest."

Some of the Psalms and wisdom literature I noted above suggest that through the awesome powers and ordering of nature, persons and communities experience not only the greatness, the power, and the goodness of God but also the radical dependence of humanity on impersonal powers beyond their control. These experiences can issue in a sense of gratitude to God for the supporting and sustaining powers of life, and in an experience of obligation to God to act and order life as stewards of the creation. Does Alston exclude these kinds of experiences of what human life is and how it ought to be governed? If they are included, could they count as evidence for a theology that does not focus so centrally on acts of God in relation to us as individual persons?

One wonders if Alston would include in his view what many contemporary theologians claim to be the experience of God as liberator from social, economic, and political oppression through the conflicts that occur in many arenas of life. The experience of God as redeemer is found in historical processes of social conflict and social change for many liberation theologians: Latin Americans, Africans and Asians, feminists, and others.

I shall not indicate further examples, but raise the question of what immediate or mediated experiences of God most support Alston's argument, and what experiences are excluded. There are experiences that could be construed as Christian that do not readily cohere with the theological argument of his article. These require a qualification of his argument.

4

The above discussion has addressed issues about the backing for Alston's argument. These issues are also of obvious importance systematically. For example, in at least some aspects of the theology of Aquinas, we humans participate in the natural law that participates in the *mind* of God, rather than participating immediately in specific divine actions. An order to all things is adduced; the requirements for a right order of life, for the true temporal ends of human life, are to be realized. One is to conform to that order or ordering, not interact with specific actions of God. Further, one wonders about the theological status of nature in Alston's chapter, of those limiting and enabling realities that exist even with reference to human action. We know that in the theological tradition, and especially some contemporary Roman Catholic theologies, nature is graced by its creator; grace is not only the individual experience of forgiveness or the newness of individual life.

The systematic tension between a theological focus on divine action and an interpretation of God in more impersonal terms has existed throughout the Western tradition. In *The Nature of the Gods*, for example, Cicero says, "There is no subject on which there is so much difference of opinion among both the learned and the ignorant," referring to "some philosophers who believe that the gods have no concern whatever with the affairs of men," and others "who believe . . . that the gods are concerned to make provision for the life of man." (Cicero does not introduce at that point the idea of divine agency defended by Alston, but I believe there is a similarity, at least, between the divine intention assumed by his second group and that made explicit by Alston.)

Many sources could be cited in which theologians have attempted to hold both the One-Beyond-the-Many, the impersonal orderer and similar ideas, together with views of the divine agency determining each particular event or being available to respond to the prayers and needs of individual human beings. Deep religious satisfaction, resonating with different experiences of the divine reality, can come from such a pluriform view. The defense of the personally caring God who responds to human petitions is possible for many Christians only because of the Christ event; indeed, among many others, Aquinas, Luther, Calvin, and H. Richard Niebuhr could move from the impersonal power that orders all things and thus is often feared (or even is the enemy) to the compassionate, loving, redeeming, responsive "Father" (and thus friend) only through what is known through Jesus Christ. Philosophically minded theologians have attempted to defend each pole of the tension, or to find ways of making a combination of them rationally persuasive. I doubt if any essentially new arguments can be made in favor of the exclusivity, or even the dominance, of either pole, just as I doubt that various current discussions will settle the tension now and for all future time. But some suggestions about why the more impersonal view is preferable are worth noting. In making them, my contrasts here are not confined to Alston's argument.

First, the position proposed by Alston is similar to various forms of Christian piety that are deeply individualistic, anthropocentric, and utilitarian. By focusing upon how God responds to individual and deeply personal petitions and needs, one often constricts the religious and moral scope of divine sovereignty and of human faithfulness to God. This is written when the press is occupied with the fate of the Kurds in Turkey, Iran, and Iraq, and with the catastrophic effects of a cyclone in Bangladesh. In the prayers of the pastor of our congregation this week at least six individuals were mentioned in the petitions for divine care, but the distant neighbors whose needs and sufferings are more numerous and at least as serious were ignored. Such constriction does not necessarily follow from a theology of God acting; it all depends on where God is "acting" and on what God is "doing." But Alston's sort of theology readily expresses and supports an individualistic pietism that has a long history in Christianity and a current vitality. If God responds to my prayers and desires and is indifferent to the fundamental needs of millions of persons in the world, I am forced to think critically about the characteristics of God and about the preoccupation with my own desires and needs.

Most comprehensive and systematic theologies have more or less rational ways to deal with natural and moral evils while insisting also on a divine responsiveness to individuals. It is not the task of this response to develop an argument in relation to the many solutions available. I can only point to the plausibility of a preference for an impersonal deity who is the source of human good, but who does not guarantee it, and who is also the source of human suffering resulting from powers beyond the control of those who suffer.

Second, Alston warns us not to rely excessively on the findings of the sciences as we think about God and God's relations to persons and to all of created life. This warning is appropriate, but it can be heeded too much. Certainly, at least since the rise of the modern sciences, "physico-theology" has been defended and attacked in the Western religious traditions. The effect on many conscientious and sensitive persons of the findings of the sciences has been the displacement of geocentric and anthropocentric views of the object of divine power, ordering, and purpose. Certainly arguments among the sciences exist in the areas of cosmology (which always invites what are functionally theological speculations), earth history, and biological evolution. Old general arguments take new precise forms as evidences are developed and theories are formulated about everything from the origins and prospective demise of life as we know it to the implications of research in genetics and the neurosciences. But it is not unreasonable to note some general lines of scientific interpretation of the place of humans within nature, and to reflect upon the relation of these ideas to the way we think about God, God's relations to all things, and what we can expect from the presence of God. It is not implausible to propose that God is the ultimate power that brings all things into being, bears down upon them, sustains them, limits them, creates the conditions of possibility for them, and determines their final destiny, as I have argued in the first volume of *Ethics from a Theocentric Perspective*.[4] The divine

4. Chicago: University of Chicago Press, 1981.

order and ordering take place through the pattern and processes of inter-
dependence of life in the world about which we learn from various sciences, and in which we participate as agents. Human life and activity are
to relate to the divine ordering, insofar as that can be discerned. Humans
are in the service of God, not God in the service of humans.

Third, developing a preference for an impersonal over an action construal of God can make a theologian heterodox, or even heretical. Supports
for such a view are drawn from an interpretation of the nature of human
experience and its context that differ from more orthodox views. They
require a revision, and partial rejection, of themes traditionally central to
Christian theology. The larger issue raised here concerns the basis for
claims of truth or plausibility in theology. This response does not attempt
to adjudicate that issue. Earlier I showed the presence of the more impersonal view within the Bible and the tradition. But a fuller development of
such a view cannot claim complete fidelity to all aspects of the Bible and
the Christian tradition. To attempt to authorize such a view by a radical
reinterpretation of traditional Christian terms and symbols smacks of intellectual dishonesty. The theologian who construes God in more impersonal terms, however, surely can ask more traditional and orthodox
colleagues what they do with the evidences and arguments that suggest
the need for theological revision. The discussion will go on between the
polarized alternatives, exploring the possible positive relation of each to
the other, as they have for centuries. There will surely be, as Cicero said,
much difference of opinion among both the learned and the ignorant.

5

This leads to my final observation and queries. Theologies that focus as
centrally on the acts of God as Alston proposes tend to lead to views
of Christian ethics that downplay the importance of order and ordering
according to structured requirements of life, to principles, and even to
rules. One of the major shifts in Protestant theological ethics in this century took place as a result of the exclusive, or at least primary, focus of
attention on the idea of the God Who Acts. For many writers in Christian
theological ethics, the fault of these views is that they lead to an excessive
occasionalism, or contextualism, in the interpretation of proper moral
choices. I shall briefly illustrate the correlation between the theology of

acts of God and interpretations of ethics. The point is this: does the theology of the God Who Acts necessarily support views of ethics that are quite occasionalistic? Does a theology of ordering by a more impersonal God cohere with an ethics that can claim more authority for laws, for proper ordering of institutions according to principles of justice, etc.?

Two influential American Protestants have taken "act language" quite seriously. The first question of ethics for Paul Lehmann and H. Richard Niebuhr is not "What ought we to do?" but "What is God doing?" For Lehmann, God is doing "humanizing" work in the world. The "theonomous conscience," graced by the redemptive work of God in and through the *koinonia,* is

> the conscience immediately sensitive to the freedom of God to do in the always changing human situation what his [i.e., God's] humanizing aims and purpose require. The *theonomous* conscience is governed and directed by the freedom of God alone. Ultimately, it is in this freedom that the decisions of men are set, and from this freedom come the power and transforming possibilities which give ethical shape to behavior.[5]

Here the idea of the God Who Acts means that God is free to do his humanizing work in very particular circumstances, and Christians are empowered to see what God in God's freedom is doing, and in a sense to get with that flow. This clearly relativizes to an extreme degree the reliability of established orders, rules, and principles, because God is not self-limited to any such perceptions of how life is to be ordered.

H. Richard Niebuhr states that "Responsibility affirms: 'God is acting in all actions upon you. So respond to all actions upon you as to respond to his action.'"[6] This is the linchpin of an ethics of the fitting, *kathekontic* ethics, which Niebuhr distinguished from teleological and deontological ethics. It takes little imagination to see how complex the process of proper response becomes. One has to *interpret* actions upon us, individually, socially, and politically (as his articles on the Second World War demonstrate) in the light of God's action. And God's action is creative, governing, judging, and redeeming. In the light of that complex interpre-

5. Paul Lehmann, *Ethics in a Christian Context* (New York: Harper and Row, 1963), 358–59.

6. H. Richard Niebuhr, *The Responsible Self* (New York: Harper and Row, 1963), 126.

tation one determines the fitting response to God's action in the circumstances, the sequence of events, etc., in which one is participating. As with Lehmann, so with H. Richard Niebuhr, the theology of the acts of God coheres with a very dynamic and somewhat open-ended view of the ethical.

My third illustration is from the ethics of Karl Barth. Barth's Christology assures us that God is gracious and God is "for man." Our actions are to testify to, endorse, respond to, etc., the gracious activity of God in each distinctive circumstance in which we hear God's command. To be sure, God will command nothing contrary to God's grace, but given the freedom of God and the specificity of God's command, we must always be open to doing something that might be contrary to the best of moral tradition, though such occasions will be rare. But it is the command of God that we are to obey. Barth charges that in moral philosophy and casuistry it is humans who determine what God commands; this violates the divine prerogative to freely command what God requires in a unique situation. I quote what is probably Barth's strongest statement of this view.

> In the demand and judgment of His command God always confronts us with a specific meaning in intention, with a will which has foreseen everything and each thing in particular, which has not left the smallest thing to chance or our caprice. The command of God as it is given to us in each moment is always and only one possibility in every conceivable particularity of its inner and outer modality. It is always a single decision, including all the thoughts and words and movements in which we execute it. We encounter it in such a way that absolutely nothing either outward or inward, either in the relative secret of our intention or in the unambiguously observable fulfillment of our actions, is left to chance or to ourselves, or rather in such a way that even in every visible or invisible detail He wills us precisely the one thing and nothing else, and measures and judges us precisely by whether we do or do not do with the same precision the one thing that He so precisely wills.[7]

My point in citing these authors is to ask whether these ethical views

7. Karl Barth, *Church Dogmatics*, II / 2, 663–64.

are necessary corollaries of the preference for a theology of the acts of God proposed by Alston. If these ethical views are unacceptable, does that fault the theology of God Who Acts? Ought one not to be concerned with this correlation between how one conceives of God and God's relations to humans and all things, and the structure or interpretation of ethics, and the norms for human activity?

This last section goes beyond Alston's chapter but from my odd sector of the theological enterprise, theological ethics, the query is not only interesting but important.

PART II

UNIVERSAL DIVINE ACTION: CREATION, HUMAN FREEDOM, AND SIN

CHAPTER 3

DIVINE ACTION, CREATED CAUSES, AND HUMAN FREEDOM

Thomas F. Tracy

Although talk of God as an actor in the drama of human history is deeply entrenched in the texts and traditions of Christianity, this language has had an uncertain career in modern theology. The sources of this problematic status are various and complex, but it is safe to say that a persistent ingredient has been worry that the notion of particular divine action is at odds with ways of describing the world that have proved their success in the natural and social sciences. So, it is often pointed out that we can and do explain events without appeal to otherworldly or supernatural agencies. And it also is said, sometimes without further argument, that if we adopt these modern modes of description and explanation, we cannot also speak of divine action within the world. Bultmann holds, for example, that we now inevitably share a scientific world-picture that leaves "no room for God's working" either in the events of the natural world or in the lives of human beings.[1] Any divine action that affects historical events, therefore, must take the form of an intervention that disrupts the intelligible structures of the world around us or threatens the coherence and integrity of our lives.

It is important to challenge the arguments that lead to these conclusions. I have argued elsewhere, for example, that we need not and should not deny that the God who creates our world might act within it to bring about events that exceed the causal powers of creatures.[2] But it is also worth considering whether God's action might be understood to guide the course of events while leaving the immanent structures of our world intact. Might it be possible, for example, to conceive of God as acting through the activity of creatures in such a way that an event can be the effect of a natural cause or the free act of a human agent and also be the intentional action of God? The theological appeal of such an account is evident; it would enable us to say, for example, that (a) the escape of the Hebrew people through the sea of reeds was both an entirely natural event and a mighty act of God in history or that (b) Augustine's conversion in the garden at Milan was both a free human action and an act of unconditional divine grace. Clearly, there are theological issues of the first order at stake here.

There is more than one way this suggestion might be developed, and in this discussion I want to explore some of the most intriguing contemporary options. I shall begin with some brief remarks on the contribution of Austin Farrer to this discussion and then turn to a recent proposal by Kathryn Tanner that puts forward a particularly strong form of the claim that the activity of created things is also the action of God. My conclusions will in part be negative; these proposals, for all their appeal, do not in the end provide quite the solutions for which we hope. But in the process of working through these issues, I shall sketch the outline of a constructive account of how we might conceive of God's action in the world.

---

1. *Jesus Christ and Mythology* (New York: Scribner's, 1958), 65. Bultmann also contends, however, that God encounters us as selves at a level beyond the reach of objective understanding. This action of God "is hidden from every eye except the eye of faith" (62).

2. E.g., "Enacting History: Ogden and Kaufman on God's Mighty Acts," *Journal of Religion* 64, no. 1 (January 1984): 20–36.

1.   The Paradox of Double Agency

In a richly imaginative and somewhat enigmatic set of lectures, Austin Farrer sketched an approach to questions about divine action that has exerted a persistent influence on Anglo-American discussions of this topic.[3] At the heart of Christian talk about God's action in the world, Farrer finds an assertion of "double agency"; that is, that a single event can be attributed to two agents, God and the creature. God acts through the operation both of impersonal natural causes and personal intentional agents, enacting the divine purposes without overriding or disrupting the activity of creatures.[4] Farrer envisions a universal and continuous divine guidance of events that is not imposed upon created things but rather is expressed in the exercise of creatures' own powers of operation. "God's agency must actually be such as to work omnipotently on, in, or through creaturely agencies without either forcing them or competing with them" (*Faith and Speculation*, 62).

Farrer affirms that we are acquainted with this divine agency at first hand in the life of faith, which is a life of friendship with God. We cannot spell out how God works in creatures, however, for when we attempt to do so, we find that double agency constitutes an unresolvable paradox: namely, "the paradox of two agents for an identical action, the one creaturely, the other divine" (104). Farrer is familiar, of course, with the suspicion that "paradox" is a dignified name for a conjunction of incompatible propositions neither of which we are prepared to give up, and he moves to quiet such misgivings. "Two agents for the same act would be indeed impossible, were they both agents in the same sense and on the same level" (104). Might we not resolve or at least ease the paradox by explaining the different senses in which and levels on which God and creatures act? Farrer thinks that this cannot be done, and there seem to be at least two considerations that motivate this conclusion.

First, Farrer insists that here we confront the limits of analogical thought about God. We cannot extend the analogy of divine action beyond certain rather general formulations, for when we do so we stumble over

3. *Faith and Speculation* (New York: New York University Press, 1967). Farrer's legacy is evident in the essays collected by Brian Hebblethwaite and Edward Henderson in *Divine Action* (Edinburgh: T and T Clark, 1990).

4. I shall follow Farrer (and ordinary language) in speaking of both things and persons as "causes" and "agents" that "act." Things stand only in relations of event-causation, while it may be that persons also operate as agent-causes in their free decisions.

the profound disanalogies between the divine and human agents. If we persist in trying to work out an account of the relation between divine and created agencies, we will find ourselves trapped in various unwanted and theologically unwholesome consequences of our familiar action concepts. The result, Farrer says, will be to "degrade [God's agency] to the creaturely level and place it in the field of interacting causalities" (62).

Second, Farrer claims that "the causal joint (so to speak) between infinite and finite action plays and in the nature of the case can play no part in our concern with God and his will" (65). The focus of attention in religious life is not on how God brings about effects in the world but on what those effects are and what they reveal to us of God's purposes. Speculation about the "mechanism" of divine action sheds no light on religious practice; we do not in this way develop or refine an ability to act in relation to God. The irrelevance of the "causal joint" to the practice of Christian life, Farrer contends, also rules it out as a subject of inquiry, for "we can think about no reality, about which we can do nothing but think."[5]

If Farrer is right in these arguments, then we can speak of God acting through the actions of creatures and yet refuse to speculate about the metaphysics of this "double agency." This would free doctrines of particular providence from the potential embarrassments of relying upon appeal to miracles.[6] It also would solve (or, more accurately, dissolve) traditional puzzles about divine grace and human freedom (66). For if the metaphysical relation of divine and created agents is beyond our conceptual reach and irrelevant to the practice of Christianity, we cannot even formulate the problem about the relation of God's action to the actions of free creatures. We can only point out that the denial of human freedom is not warranted by an affirmation of the universality and sovereignty of God's gracious will.

Are the two arguments Farrer has given sufficient to establish these conclusions? I think not, though Farrer is right that there are profound limits on our ability to construct an account of God's relation to the world in action. With regard to the danger of being ensnared by our analogies, the key question is whether there are logical requirements associated

---

5. P. 171. Farrer was writing in the early 1960s and was responding, in part, to logical positivism. The question about the "causal joint" has the look of a metaphysical quagmire, and Farrer responded by posting its boundaries and warning us away.

6. Farrer does not deny, however, that God might act outside the ordinary course of nature.

with the concept of an agent that have theologically problematic consequences if we attempt to meet these requirements in a consistently developed account of divine agency. For example, if we speak of God as an agent, is it necessary also to speak of God as existing in time or as embodied or as limited by the active powers of other agents? These questions are difficult to answer for a number of reasons: because concepts do not come with fixed sets of necessary conditions for their use, because it is not always clear what is contained in the meaning of a term and what happens to be true of its standard instances, and because it is open to us to modify the rules for use of a term and thereby generate related but distinct senses.[7] It is also a matter of dispute as to which conceptual consequences of our action concepts are theologically inadmissible. Clearly, it is going to be difficult to say in advance how fully we can elaborate a conception of God as agent before we run into theological trouble. An argument must be made for the general conclusion that any attempt to resolve the paradox of double agency will inevitably "degrade God's agency to the creaturely level." Otherwise, we can and should continue the inquiry.

With regard to Farrer's second argument, I think that he is right about the inaccessibility of the "causal joint" between divine and created agencies, but wrong in concluding from this that we cannot and need not attempt further explication of double agency. It is helpful here to distinguish two respects in which we might inquire about *how* an agent acts. First, we may simply be asking for a more detailed account of *what* the agent has done or is doing. If we want to know how Eusebius caused the banishment of his theological opponent Athanasius, we are inquiring about what he did in order to produce this result. Complex actions of this sort are organized into instrumental hierarchies in which an agent does one thing in order to do another; for example, Eusebius convinced Constantine that Athanasius was politically dangerous, he did so by spreading rumors that Athanasius had threatened to interrupt grain shipments from Alexandria, and he spread the rumors by speaking to influential friends, and so on. The regress "down" an instrumental action series must come to an end at some point, however, and it can do so only in an action that an agent undertakes without having to perform any intentionally prior action as a means to this end. Such an action is "basic." There

7. For helpful discussion of these issues see Alston, "Divine and Human Action," in *Divine and Human Action*, ed. T. Morris (Ithaca, N.Y.: Cornell University Press, 1988).

is disagreement, as one might expect, about what sorts of actions are basic for human agents, but for my purposes it is enough to note that when we reach this level the question about *how* the agent acts has a significantly different force. Here we are asking about the agent's capacity to perform intentional actions at all rather than about how the agent carries out her intentions, and this constitutes a *second* type of question about how an agent acts.

There are significant limitations on our ability to answer either of these "how-questions" when we raise them about the acts of God. Farrer is on firmest ground in contending that we face intrinsic conceptual limits when we attempt to answer questions of the second type. We cannot say how God brings about the effects that we take to be God's basic actions (whatever these may be), because we have so limited a grasp upon what it is to be the divine agent. I have argued elsewhere that we can conceive of God as "the perfection of agency."[8] This involves extending the concept of an agent of intentional actions beyond its familiar instances, stripping away the limitations that attach to finite agents (including, for example, the limitations associated with embodiment). This process, I contend, does not break down the basic logical structure of the concept; we can coherently affirm *that* God is an agent. But it does leave us unable to spell out *what* it is to be such an agent and to act as this agent acts. We are left only with various partial analogies to guide the imagination toward a mode of agency that vastly exceeds our own.

There remain, however, questions of the first type; here inquiry about how God acts calls for an answer that moves down the instrumental structure of the divine action, explaining what God does in order to realize the higher level purposes (e.g., establishing a covenant with Israel) that we ascribe to the divine agency.[9] There are good reasons for reticence about claiming to understand the deeper substructure of God's action in the world. Given our epistemic limitations as creatures, we cannot expect to grasp the full content of God's activity. First, God acts with a scope (over all creatures) and an intimacy (to every creature) that exceeds our capacities of understanding. Second, God's overarching purposes can be achieved through an inexhaustibly rich variety of particular strategies of action, some of which we may discern but most of which we must acknowledge we do not. Third, to this unavoidable incompleteness in our

---

8. See *God, Action, and Embodiment* (Grand Rapids, Mich.: Eerdmans, 1984).

9. One way to handle this question, as we will see in a moment, is to hold that all of God's actions are basic, so that there is no instrumental substructure to the divine action.

grasp of God's activity, we must add the actual limits of our knowledge about what God has created; our ability to construct an account of God's action in the world is constrained by our limited understanding of the world in which God acts.

These epistemic limits, however, do not altogether release us from the task of explaining how (in the second sense) we understand God to act. If we claim that God acts with particular purposes in history (e.g., to rescue the Hebrew people from captivity in Egypt), then we must affirm that there is some *way* in which God does this. How detailed an account can or should we try to give of the ways of God in the world? The most we can expect, I think, is to make the case that there is *some* structure of action, coherent with the rest of what we believe about the world, by which the divine agent might bring about the kinds of higher order acts that we have come (e.g., through reflection on biblical texts and the traditions of theological interpretation) to attribute to God. It may well be (as I shall contend below) that we can conceive of a number of means by which God could achieve these ends, including more than one type of action that might be basic for God. If there is no compelling reason to settle on one account rather than another, then we need not embrace any single answer to the first question about how God acts. But we do not have good grounds simply to "refuse the challenge," as Farrer puts it (*Faith and Speculation*, 62), of explaining what we mean when we say that God acts in and through creatures.

2.   Divine Action and Created Causes

Within these limits, the way remains open for an exploration of the relation between divine and created agencies, and we may hope to shed some further light on the notion of double agency. A natural point at which to begin the discussion is with God's activity as creator. In what sense or senses can we say that God, by virtue of initiating and sustaining the existence of finite agencies, is the agent of their acts?

A. Direct Divine Action

I want to begin with a recent proposal that puts forward an especially thoroughgoing version of the claim that God acts in the activity of creatures. In a complex and fascinating book, Kathryn Tanner takes up the task of establishing the logical consistency of the claims that

1. "a radically transcendent God exercises a universal and uncondi- tional agency,"
2. created things possess "their own power and efficacy,"
3. human beings are "free and therefore responsible for the character of their own lives."[10]

The characteristic modern response to these claims, Tanner suggests, is to find them contradictory and to resolve the inconsistency by weakening one or more of them, typically the first. She will have none of this strategy, and insists instead on the strongest possible reading of the first claim.

> God's agency must be talked about as universal and immediate, . . . conversely, everything non-divine must be talked about as existing in a relation of total and immediate dependence upon God. (84)

> A created cause can be said to bring about a certain created effect by its own power, or a created agency can be talked about as freely intending the object of its rational volition, only if God is said to found that causality or agency directly and *in toto*—in power, exercise, manner of activity and effect. (86)

The dependence of created things upon God is universal and total; every event in the career of every creature depends upon God's creative agency. Further, this dependence is also direct, or immediate; "God must not be talked about as only indirectly efficacious of the whole in virtue of intermediate agencies" (82). We can put this point in the terms used above in discussing complex intentional actions: there is no instrumental substructure in God's creative activity, God does not do one thing by doing another. Each event that is caused by God is brought about di- rectly, that is, as a basic action. It follows that God does not act *by means of* second causes, bringing about a finite effect by establishing the causal

10. *God and Creation in Christian Theology: Tyranny or Empowerment?* (Oxford: Basil Blackwell, 1988), 1–2. Tanner argues not only for the logical consistency of these propositions but also for their systematic coherence, i.e., their mutual implication (see, e.g., 82).

series that includes it. Rather, God produces the effect directly, as God does each member of the causal chain to which it belongs. On this account, God does not cooperate with, influence, or affect the actions of creatures; rather, God enacts them (see 93–96). There is, then, an internal connection between the claim that God's agency is immediate and the claim that God is always the total cause of each created event.

This understanding of God's creative agency certainly allows us to say that the acts of creatures are also God's acts. But is it consistent with the other two of Tanner's initial three propositions? In the remainder of this section, I consider the compatibility of universal *direct* divine action with the claim that creatures exercise their own causal powers.[11] In the next section, on *indirect* divine action, I explore some alternatives to Tanner's account of God's agency that are more clearly consistent with strong claims about creaturely causality. I then turn to issues raised by the claim that human agents possess the particular sort of causal power required for *free* intentional action.

It appears that if God is the immediate cause of every finite event, then creatures cannot be causes in the sense that Tanner proposes; namely, that they possess and exercise "their own power and efficacy." Suppose we understand an event as a state of affairs in which an individual (i) possesses a property (P) at a time (t).[12] Then for any causal sequence in the world, God immediately brings about not only the existence of the individuals (i_1 and i_2) involved in it, but also the events of i_1 being P_1 at t_1 and i_2 being P_2 at t_2. When a baseball breaks a window, God *directly* causes both the event of the ball having a certain direction and velocity at t_1 and the event of the glass shattering at t_2. It appears that all of the causal work in this sequence is done by God. The two finite events can be causally related in the sense that they stand in certain regular relations to each other; for example, as Humean patterns of temporally ordered constant conjunction or as belonging to complex networks of counterfactuals. But the only "power and efficacy" exercised here is that which attaches to the divine agency, and so it appears that God is not only the universal cause but also the *only* cause, at least in the strong sense that Tanner

11. My discussion of this objection is indebted to a response by Marilyn Adams ("Divine Creation and Transcendence vs. Created Causal Power") to the paper by Tanner ("God's Unconditional Efficacy and Human Freedom to Do Otherwise") given at the original UCLA conference from which most of the essays in this volume come.

12. Cf. Philip Quinn, "Divine Conservation, Secondary Causes, and Occasionalism," in Morris, *Divine and Human Action*, 52.

intends. The activity of the creature, on such an account, is merely the occasion for God's action of directly producing the effect, and so this type of view has long been called "occasionalism."

It is clear that Tanner means to avoid this result, and she deploys a set of interrelated considerations in trying to do so. First, she contends that if creatures exist in total and immediate dependence upon God, then any property they possess is received through this direct divine agency. "Created power and efficacy just become cases of created being existing in a total and immediate dependence upon the God who brings to be" (*God and Creation*, 85). If this claim is made without further argument, however, it simply begs the question. While classical theists do affirm that whatever active powers a creature possesses it has from the hand of God, it does not follow that absolutely any form of divine action will be compatible with the exercise by creatures of genuine causal powers. The objection to Tanner's position is precisely that her particular account of God's agency (namely, as universally direct) is not compatible with the efficacy of created causes.

Tanner recognizes this difficulty and goes on to introduce a further consideration.

> The theologian talks of an ordered nexus of created causes and effects in a relation of total and immediate dependence upon divine agency. Two different orders of efficacy become evident: along a "horizontal" plane, an order of created causes and effects; along a "vertical" plane, the order whereby God founds the former. Predicates applied to created beings . . . can be understood to hold simply within the horizontal plane of relations among created beings. . . . Ascribing them to created beings cannot run contrary, then, to our rules for talk of God's agency and the creature. (89–90)

This distinction of levels is helpful in addressing questions about contingency and human freedom, and I shall return to it below. But it is of no help at all on the problem about the causal powers of creatures. For here the question is whether, given this particular account of God's activity on the vertical axis, it is possible to affirm the causal efficacy of creatures on the horizontal axis. Unless this argument is supplemented in some way, it amounts simply to a reassertion of the claim that the exercise of genuine causal powers is among the properties that God directly enacts in creatures.

Underlying these two arguments, and at the heart of Tanner's position, is the claim that the worry about occasionalism results from a theologically defective, "contrastive" understanding of God's transcendence. Transcendence must not be defined in terms of contrasts between divine and nondivine being or agency, for this imprisons God within boundaries set by the terms of the contrast and so makes God finite. A noncontrastive understanding of transcendence avoids this paradoxical result by affirming that God transcends the very distinctions by which we try to mark off the divine from the nondivine. "It is the mutual exclusiveness of *all* apparent antitheses . . . which must give way before such a God" (79).

Tanner claims that if we understand God's transcendence in this way, then there can be no question of God's agency displacing the real causal relations of creatures. It is not entirely clear how this argument should go, but let me offer a rough approximation. The charge that Tanner's position leads to occasionalism trades upon the contrasts by which we ordinarily distinguish the activity of causal agents. The objector holds that if, for some effect, some causal agent is the immediate cause (in the sense of operating without intermediaries) and total cause (in the sense that the effect is brought about in its entirety by this agent's activity), then there can only be one such cause and no other agent can play this causal role in the production of this effect. Given a noncontrastive understanding of the divine transcendence, however, we should deny that this way of distinguishing agents and their causal roles applies to God's relation to creatures. When the activity of a creature is the cause of an effect, that effect in its entirety can also be attributed to God. The operation of the finite agent is the sufficient condition of its effect within the order of created causes on the horizontal level. But God's transcendent agency is sufficient for the existence *and operation* of the cause, and for the existence *and character* of the effect. Here we have double agency in the strongest possible sense.

Is this convincing as a reply to the worry about occasionalism? The idea of noncontrastive transcendence contains an important theological insight, but Tanner's formulation of that idea faces fatal objections. It cannot be the case that God transcends *all* contrasts, though Tanner speaks this way. [13] At the very least, a contrast is asserted between beings that are defined by some particular network of contrasts and that Being who cannot be so defined. Further, the concept of such a Being is para-

13. See, for example, her claim that God "is not characterized by contrast with any sort of being" (46).

doxical if defined in terms of contrasts as such (namely, the Being, in contrast to all other beings, who cannot be defined by contrasts) rather than in terms of some particular contrast or set of contrasts. So it cannot be the case that establishing a contrast between God and the world inevitably leads to treating God as one limited being among others. Some contrasts may have this consequence, others will not. Generally speaking, we should not be so eager to contrast God and world that we leave ourselves puzzled by how they can be related; the relation, and a very specific one according to Christianity, is primary. But this means that we should be careful about *which* contrasts we draw, not that we should say that God transcends all contrasts. A further argument must then be made that the contrast in question, namely, the very basic contrast at work in differentiating the causal roles of distinct agents, is sufficiently problematic for theology that we must pay the price in intelligibility that is involved in giving it up.

B. Indirect Divine Action

If we affirm that creatures exercise genuine causal powers, there are compelling conceptual reasons to deny that God is the direct and total cause of every finite event. The evident alternative is to say that those effects that flow from the causal activity of creatures are *indirect* results of divine agency; here God acts by means of finite causes, bringing about effects through created intermediaries. This claim is entirely compatible with the assertion that (1) creaturely effects can be counted as God's acts, so that we can continue to speak of double agency, and even that (2) every effect of finite causes can be attributed to God's agency. Let me briefly develop each of these points.

When an agent intentionally brings about an effect by making use of some instrument or intermediary, we ordinarily ascribe that effect (under some limited subset of the descriptions that are true of it) to the agent as his or her act. So we say both that the forester splits the log and that the axe splits the log. A single event (the log's being split) is ascribed to two causal agents, but we can distinguish the causal contribution of each to their joint effect: the forester swings the axe and the axe strikes the log. In such a case an intentional agent works by means of the passive and active causal powers of an instrumental agent. God's causal activity goes much deeper, of course, because God brings about and sustains the very existence of finite causes themselves. But in addition to this direct divine agency, events that flow from the network of finite causes that God has established can be attributed to God as indirect divine acts.[14] God brings about these events by bringing about creatures that produce them. No doubt God could, if God chose, bring about these effects directly; say, God could cause there suddenly to be a magnificent oak tree, growth rings and all, in the midst of a previously empty field. But the presence of the oak tree is no less God's act because it is the result of an extended causal series that includes a squirrel burying an acorn that takes root and grows for a hundred years.

We can, if we wish, generate a story about God's relation to finite causes according to which *everything* that creatures do is also done by God. This will be the result if we imagine, for example, that God establishes a universally deterministic order of created causes. In order to keep this picture simple, we shall suppose that this created order has an absolute beginning. God directly brings about the existence of some initial set of creatures, and God directly sustains (conserves) the existence of these individuals and their causal descendants. God's creative activity is continuous, therefore, in the sense that if at any time God does not act to conserve the existence of a creature, that individual will cease to be.[15] By choosing which individuals constitute the "first generation" of created things, God determines what causal powers will be set at work in the world; most creatures will possess both active and passive causal powers, that is, capacities both to affect other entities and to be affected by them. In this way God directly sets the initial conditions and the general laws of this created order. Beyond the opening moment of creation, however, God does not (ordinarily) directly determine particular events in the world. Rather, the properties that an individual possesses at any time will be determined by its interactions with other creatures.[16] So, God's

14. See William Alston, "God's Action in the World," in *Evolution and Creation*, ed. Ernan McMullin (Notre Dame, Ind.: University of Notre Dame Press, 1985), 200–202.

15. Perhaps this picture should include a distinction between "basic individuals," which are the fundamental constituents of things, and "complex individuals," which consist in or depend upon relatively stable organizations of basic individuals. Then God's conservation of basic individuals will be direct while God's conservation of complex individuals will be both direct (in sustaining their constituent basic individuals) and indirect (in instituting a causal order that generates this organization of basic individuals).

16. It might be argued that if God directly causes the *existence* of an individual then God must directly cause that individual *to possess each of its properties*. This might be thought to follow from the premise that God cannot cause bare existence, but must cause the existence

direct action in the creation and conservation of a world of finite causal agents *indirectly* determines each event that will occur in that world over the course of its history.

Here we have a picture of divine and created agencies that both preserves the genuine causal powers of creatures and presents a strong understanding of the dependence of every event on God's agency. God is the universal cause; every event is the enactment of God's unfrustratable intention for it. Further, we can say that God is the total cause in the sense that (a) every aspect of every creature's career is determined by God's agency, and (b) creatures ultimately depend upon God alone, since their proximate created causes are themselves grounded in God's action.

It is worth pressing a bit farther with this metaphysical storytelling in order to illustrate an additional point. Suppose we abandon, as I think we should, the simple determinism of the picture I just sketched. Let us assume instead that the world includes events that are instances of

---

of something in particular. Consider, however, the following two propositions (where i is an individual, P is a property, and t is a time):

1. God directly causes i to exist at t
2. i is P at t.

Without the addition of further premises, the conjunction of (1) and (2) does not entail

3. God directly causes i to be P at t.

God causes the individual, with all its properties, to exist. But God may act indirectly (i.e., through secondary causes) to bring it about that i is P at t, or God may permit a finite free agent to bring this about.

Can we find additional premises that, in conjunction with (1) and (2), would entail (3)? One possibility is the following:

4. P is an essential property of i.

(1) and (4) *entail* (2); God cannot cause i (as opposed to some other individual) to exist unless i is P. But could the causal route by which i is P be left open? It appears not, for if God indirectly brings it about that i is P, then God indirectly brings about the existence of i. Conversely, if God directly causes the existence of i, and if P is an essential property of i, then God must directly cause i to be P.

The flaw in this argument is that it slides between different senses of "causing to exist." First, there is causing to be ex nihilo, which God alone does and which is not a species of change, since there is nothing to change until God creates. Second, there is causing to be this rather than that. Creaturely causes bring about changes in existing things, and therefore can cause particular complex individuals "to come into existence" or "to cease to exist," as in birth and death. God is the direct cause of existence, in the first sense, of anything that exists. But God may be the indirect cause of existence, in the second sense, of finite things produced within the causal structures of the world that God causes to be. So it does not follow that if God is the direct cause of the existence of i, then God is the direct cause of i being P, even if P is essential to i. Similarly, God may permit finite agents to determine some of their own properties in free actions, though God causes (in the first sense) the existence of the free act and of the agent that performs it.

indeterministic chance; that is, events that are not simply unpredictable for us by virtue of the complexity of the causal factors that produce them (for example, as in a deterministic mechanism of randomization), but that are not determined by the prior history of the universe nor by the free choice of any created agent. Since current physical theory gives a prominent place to such events at the lower reaches of the world's organization, and since these events can have significant effects on the macroscopic level (for example, when they are amplified in various ways), there is good reason to consider them. It is open to the theist to think of such events as directly brought about by God. They occur by chance, then, on the "horizontal" level in their relation to other events in the world, but they are directly determined by God's agency "vertically."[17] In this way God would have a continuous direct involvement with the development of the world's history, in addition to God's indirect involvement through creaturely agencies. And this direct contribution to the shape of events would not take the form of a "miraculous" departure from the ordinary course of nature, since this form of divine action is compatible with anything the natural sciences might tell us about the regular distribution of such events in probabilistic patterns. God's providential governance of the world's history, therefore, need not be identified solely with God's initial ordering of creaturely causal processes (which simply run the program that God has written into them) or with special direct "interventions" that momentarily suspend those processes. A world of this sort is characterized both by reliable causal structures and by an inherent openness to novelty, and so can include genuine creaturely causality as well as continuous divine involvement in shaping the course of events at its foundation.

My concern so far has been to see how strong an account we might

---

17. Might some created events occur by chance not only with regard to creaturely causes but also with respect to the divine cause? If there are such events then (*contra* Einstein) God really does play dice with the universe. There is an apparent paradox, however, in the idea that God causes there to be events that do not have a sufficient cause. Insofar as *we* bring about chance events, we do so *indirectly*, i.e., by setting up some mechanism that generates results which we cannot predict. But in this case we are not dealing with indeterministic chance, only with the limits of our understanding of the natural order or with complexity that exceeds our calculative abilities. This, of course, is not a possibility for God. If we were to devise a mechanism that generates genuinely chance results, it would have to exploit already existing structures of indeterministic change. But this too is not an option for God. Perhaps God can indirectly bring about chance events by establishing structures of indeterministic interaction between created things. Or perhaps God can create chance events directly, by willing that one of a set of events occur without specifying which. Peter van Inwagen thinks that this is possible;

give of God's agency in the creature if we give up the claim that every
event is a direct, or basic, act of God. Every event will be God's act, I
have argued, in a world in which effects follow with necessity from chains
of events that are rooted in God's direct action of initiating an order
of created causes. Even a world that includes chance events, while not
deterministic in its structure "horizontally," may nonetheless be determined in all of its operations by God. In worlds of these types, everything
the creature does is also done by God, though the causal roles of God
and creatures can always be distinguished.

There are good reasons, however, to resist a divine determinism of
this sort. Christians typically have wished to affirm that human beings
come from God's hand in possession of whatever freedom is required
for responsible moral choice, and it can be argued that universal divine
determinism is incompatible with such freedom. Further, if we embrace
divine determinism, then it is very difficult to avoid the conclusion *all*
human actions—those of Joseph Mengele at Auschwitz no less than those
of Saint Francis of Assisi—can be ascribed to the divine will. I want to
turn, then, from the general question of creaturely causality to the particular question of human freedom.

3.   Divine Action and Human Freedom

A.   Direct Causation of Free Acts

Can free human acts also be regarded as God's acts? It will be helpful to
return briefly to Tanner's position. If it is correct to conclude that Tanner's account of God's agency is incompatible with the exercise by creatures of genuine causal powers, then clearly human beings cannot be free
agents of intentional actions; indeed, there will be no finite intentional
agents at all. But let us suppose that this account does permit creatures
to possess their own causal powers. Does it also permit human freedom?
On this account, the free act of a created agent is the immediate effect of
God's action, just as is the operation of a created cause. Once again, it
is not enough simply to assert this; we want to know whether a free human

---

see "The Place of Chance in a World Sustained by God," in Morris, *Divine and Human Action*, 229.

act *can* be the immediate effect of divine agency. Tanner appeals to the distinction between the levels on which God and creatures act, contending that questions about human freedom (a) concern only the relation of our actions to other events on the horizontal level, and therefore (b) are entirely unaffected by claims about God's creative agency on the vertical axis. "There need be no contradiction in saying relations that are free or contingent along the horizontal axis of a created order are determined to be so in a vertical relation of absolute dependence upon divine agency" (*God and Creation*, 90).

This suggests the possibility of combining a strong (i.e., incompatibilist) account of human freedom in the created order with a thoroughgoing insistence upon the universality, immediacy, and sufficiency of God's agency. We might hold that an agent S is free in intentionally undertaking action A at time t only if S's doing A at t is not causally necessitated by the world's history (including the actions of other created free agents) prior to t. An event E is causally necessitated if the proposition "E occurs" is entailed by a conjunction of true propositions describing (a) causally relevant antecedent events and (b) laws of nature.[18] The event of S freely doing A at t will have various necessary conditions in the world's history prior to t, but it will not have causally sufficient conditions; given this causal history, S is able either to do A or to refrain from doing A. Having said this, we can also affirm that S's doing A at t is the immediate effect of God's activity. For while God has established a created order within which S's decision about A is not necessitated by the history of the *world* prior to t, it may nonetheless be the case that *God* brings it about that S does A at t. As long as God does so *directly*, rather than through any series of creaturely intermediaries, the divine agency will not violate this necessary (but not sufficient) condition for human freedom.

There are two forms that this direct divine causation of human action might be thought to take. The strongest would claim that the free acts of

---

18. Questions about foreknowledge and freedom crop up here in the form of a problem about prophecy. Suppose God enables a human being to prophesy that some other human agent S will freely do A at t. Then there is a true proposition about the world prior to t that, together with the right sorts of necessary truths (e.g., "Necessarily, God does not lie"; "Necessarily, if God causes someone to prophesy that an event E will occur, then E will occur") entails that S does A at t. But the state of affairs that satisfies the proposition "S utters the true prophecy that S will choose to do A at t" is not, I would argue, *causally* relevant to the occurrence of S doing A. Obviously, there is more to be said about the problem of foreknowledge and freedom.

human agents are themselves enacted by God as basic divine actions; when a person S undertakes a basic action A, God directly brings A about. This is not simply to say that the act is overdetermined. Two intentional agents may together produce an effect by each acting in a way that would, by itself, be sufficient to secure the result. In a case of that sort, we can distinguish the basic act of each agent. By contrast, God's direct causation of human action (on this first account) requires that a *single instance* of basic action be undertaken by more than one agent; the very act that is initiated by S is simultaneously initiated by God. This is a very puzzling notion. Ordinarily, any single instance of basic action is ascribed to only one agent. If we were to attribute a single basic action to two agents, we could not differentiate the agents by distinguishing what they do. So, if God performs the basic actions of *every* created intentional agent, there will be no way to distinguish created agents from God; that is, there will be no created agents at all.

One might make what at least appears to be a weaker claim: that what God directly brings about is not the action A but rather the performance of A by the finite agent S. God acts directly in causing S to do A, but God acts indirectly in causing A. This allows us to distinguish the basic acts performed by God and the creature. If we think of basic action as a two-place relation of "undertaking" between individual agents and instances of act-types, then we can express the human agent's basic action as "S undertakes A" and God's basic action as "God undertakes 'S undertakes A.'" In the discussion that follows, I shall focus on this version of the claim that God directly causes free human acts.

Does this understanding of the universal sufficiency of God's agency (which I shall call "omnicausality") affirm human freedom on the horizontal level only to rescind it on the vertical level of relation to God? Although our free actions do not follow with necessity from the past history of the world, they *do* follow with necessity from God's act of willing that we undertake them. For God's agency necessarily achieves what it wills, and (on this account) God's will includes each of my choices. If we share the incompatibilist intuition that an action cannot be free if it is necessitated by its causal antecedents in the world, then there appear to be equally compelling reasons to deny that free human actions are necessitated by the divine will.

To this objection, proponents of divine omnicausality might offer the following reply.[19] "You theological incompatibilists worry that God's act of directly bringing it about that S does A renders the event of S doing A necessary, and therefore unfree. But this conclusion is mistaken, since it trades upon an inference of the following type.

1. Necessarily, if God wills that some event E occur, then E occurs.
2. God wills that E occur.
3. Necessarily, E occurs.

This argument involves a modal fallacy; from these premises it follows only that E occurs, not that it is necessary that E occur. In order to reach the stronger conclusion, we would need to modify the second premise:

2′. Necessarily, God wills that E.

But this is not a claim that an advocate of divine omnicausality needs to make, nor is it a theologically promising position, since for many substitutions for E (e.g., statements about the existence and activity of creatures) it restricts God's freedom in a way that the vast majority of theologians have wanted to avoid. So if God wills that S do A at t, then S does A at t, but we need not deny the contingency, and with it the freedom, of S's action."

All of this is logically correct, but it does not directly meet the problem posed by the incompatibilist. The latter is concerned not only with metaphysical necessity and contingency (with whether there is at least one possible world that does not include the event of S doing A at t), but also with causal necessity and contingency (with whether the event of S doing A at t has causally sufficient conditions in the actual world). The theological incompatibilist contends that if God directly causes the human agent's act, then that act is a metaphysically contingent causally determined event rather than a metaphysically contingent causally undetermined event, and so is not free. In order to express the theological incompatibilist's point, we must reformulate our earlier statement of the key necessary condition for freedom so that it excludes determination not only by other

19. See Tanner's discussion of the necessary efficacy of God's will (in *God and Creation*, 73–76, and chapter 4 of this volume). In an intriguing essay, William Mann makes a similar argument: see "God's Freedom, Human Freedom, and God's Responsibility for Sin," in Morris, *Divine and Human Action*, 204–5. Also see Thomas Aquinas, *Summa Theologica*, I–II, 10, 4, ad 3, and compare I, 19, 8 and 22, 4.

created agents but also by the divine agent. If an agent's performance of an intentional action is free, then "S chooses to do A at t" cannot be entailed by true propositions describing the laws of nature and the history of the world prior to t nor by true propositions about the causally relevant actions of any other agent. But given (1) above, God's willing that S choose to do A at t entails S choosing A at t. There is no modal fallacy here, but given the incompatibilist's understanding of freedom, S is not free with regard to A at t.

In light of these considerations, the idea of divine omnicausality appears to leave us with a theological compatibilism; that is, the view that human freedom, in an appropriately restricted sense, is compatible with divine determination.[20] There are two senses, on this account, in which we may speak of free human action. First, this vertical determinism can be combined, as we have seen, with a horizontal incompatibilism. We can then say that God is the direct cause of free human actions, in the sense that these actions (though determined by God) are free with regard to their creaturely antecedents. Second, the vertical determinism may be "softened" by pointing out that our actions are free in the sense that God does not act as an external power that coerces or constrains us to act against our will; we do what we will, though what we will is determined by God.

The theological incompatibilist will not find this account of freedom

20. Does the derivation of determinism from divine omnicausality reflect a failure to qualify appropriately the analogy of action in its theological use? It is worth recalling here Farrer's claim that we will generate intractable difficulties about the relation of divine and created agency if we carry over in talk of God too much of our familiar patterns of speech about action and causation. The issues raised here are complex, but let me simply note two points. First, we need to make use here of only the most abstract and formal notion of agency: that God intentionally brings about certain states of affairs. The worry about determinism is triggered by the claim that this divine "bringing about" is *sufficient* for its effect when that effect is a free act. However mysterious the nature of God's activity and however inadequate our analogies for it, if we affirm its universal sufficiency, we logically cannot affirm that creatures are free in the full incompatibilist sense. For *no* agent can be the sufficient cause of another agent's free act. Second, it follows that appeal to the analogical character of our talk about God will not enable us to affirm divine omnicausality but avoid determinism. We could say that when we attribute agency and causality to God we do so in a special sense; we attribute not agency, but rather a property of agency-likeness that we cannot spell out except to say that this divine "agency" is the sufficient "cause" of its effects without necessitating them. But it is not only (or primarily) the concepts of agency and causation that shift in meaning here; talk of sufficiency and necessity is rendered utterly opaque. At this point, analogical usage appears to collapse into equivocation.

sufficiently strong. The key considerations in this disagreement are theological, rather than questions of philosophical action theory. The incompatibilist is concerned that theological determinism both (a) denies certain great goods in human moral life and relation to God and (b) makes God the cause of sin. The theological compatibilist, on the other hand, may worry that a stronger understanding of human freedom both (a) carries with it a Pelagian or semi-Pelagian understanding of divine grace,[21] and (b) lacks the resources to give a sufficiently strong account of divine sovereignty and providence.

It is not my intention to carry out this debate here, but only to argue that the concept of double agency does not, after all, release us from it. The idea of double agency, as we first encountered it, seemed to provide an ideal vehicle for explicating the claim that a single event (say, of an individual turning to God in repentance and love) is both a free human act and God's direct action. But if my arguments here are correct, we must continue to grapple with the mutually limiting character of claims about human freedom and divine agency. If our acts are directly enacted by God, then there is an important sense in which they are not free, and if they are free in this strong sense, then they cannot be direct acts of God. The idea of double agency does not, in the end, provide us with a satisfying resolution of the long-standing debate over the theological significance of incompatibilist freedom.

B. Indirect Causation of Free Acts: Limited Double Agency

If we affirm incompatibilist freedom, is there *any* sense in which we can speak of divine agency in free human acts? I want to conclude by arguing briefly that there are several such senses and that these forms of double agency, while more limited than those so far considered, have important theological work to do.

There are a number of familiar circumstances in which a single event

21. It is worth noting that an affirmation of incompatibilist freedom does not *entail* Pelagianism (or semi-Pelagianism); indeed, it is logically possible to affirm both that (1) human agents possess this freedom in at least some of their actions and (2) salvation is *not* contingent upon free human choices.

may be regarded as the free act of more than one intentional agent. First, two or more agents may combine their causal powers to bring about a shared result, either as separately insufficient but jointly sufficient causes or as redundant, overdetermining causes; you and I together roll a stone out of the roadway, perhaps each applying force sufficient to move it. Second, one agent may act on behalf of another, serving, we might say, as that agent's agent; when the presidential spokesman states the president's position, we say that the president has stated his position. Third, one agent may play so crucial a role in enabling or inducing another agent to act that we attribute the act to both agents; you might, by argument, force of example, and affection lead me to make some positive change in the way I live, and I might say that this change is as much your accomplishment as mine. Cases of this third kind can become quite complex, raising subtle questions about responsibility and generating an intriguing asymmetry between instances in which the recipient agent responds positively (and credits the initiating agent) and those in which the agent responds negatively (and accepts or is assigned the responsibility himself).[22]

The claim of double agency is limited in each of these cases by virtue of the fact that we can distinguish what the two agents do even though we attribute a single action to them. Specifically, we acknowledge that the agents involved perform distinct *basic* actions. In the first case, the agents each undertake basic actions that initiate instrumental series involving causal chains that converge in the production of a common effect. In the second and third cases, one agent's basic act is undertaken with the intention of setting in motion an instrumental series that includes another agent's free basic act.

These forms of limited double agency provide useful analogical patterns for thinking about God's action in the actions of free creatures, and each has in fact been called upon in the devotional and theological language of Christianity. A variety of the first is employed in talk of God acting providentially to bring about, as a consequence of human action, a good that the human agent did not intend or does not have the power to achieve. The second is called upon in understanding cer-

---

22. This asymmetry of responsibility is most extreme in considering God's solicitation of our good and our response in love, and it is helpful (though I do not think it sufficient) in dealing with questions about divine grace and human freedom.

tain human utterances to be performatives that enact God's intentions: for example, a prophet declares God's judgment or mercy; a priest or minister undertakes liturgical and sacramental acts that make God's promises effective here and now (as when the forgiveness of sin is declared in God's name).[23] The third provides a key pattern for conceiving of the action of God in guiding the development of individual lives, as we see, for example, in Augustine's *Confessions*. Here double agency is exercised by shaping the orienting conditions under which an agent acts. Clearly, God's agency plays a unique role in this respect; God is not simply a particular contributor to the context of free action but rather creates, conserves, and governs the finite causal nexus as a whole. I want to develop this third point briefly; in order to do so it will be helpful to say a bit more about creaturely freedom.

Human freedom, on any plausible account, operates in a causal context that limits and focuses the agent's choices. An unadorned statement of an incompatibilist criterion for free will can be seriously misleading, since it states only the barest necessary condition for a strong conception of freedom and may leave the impression that our choices are not only undetermined but also largely unconditioned. If we do possess incompatibilist freedom, it can only consist in a capacity to introduce a restricted range of creative variations in the midst of causal structures that are given for us. So, our capacity for voluntary action depends upon underlying processes of bodily life that we do not choose or intentionally undertake, and it is exercised amid the hard necessities of the natural world. Further, our actions are conceived and undertaken in a complex motivational context that includes not only our immediate physical circumstances and present beliefs but also memory of past experience and action (much of which is beyond the reach of easy recall), deeply rooted patterns of emotional response, habits and inclinations, and so on. The incompatibilist claims that these orienting conditions of action do not exhaustively determine those of our choices that are free. They do, however, constitute material with which we must work in determining our act. Our freedom, then, can only consist in a capacity to make something new of what is given for us, and the possibilities for what we make are structured by what is given.

23. Ronald Thiemann discusses the example of liturgical pardon in *Revelation and Theology: The Gospel as Narrated Promise* (Notre Dame, Ind.: Notre Dame University Press, 1985), 106.

On the theist's account, this creaturely freedom and its causal context exist by God's action and permission. God not only establishes the agent's capacity for free action, God also plays a unique role in setting the conditions under which that capacity is exercised. I noted earlier that we can properly regard events as indirect acts of God if they occur within the right sorts of causal chains rooted in God's direct action. Since our operation as agents depends massively upon natural regularities (which both constitute us as organisms and establish the stable environment in which we act), our action everywhere presupposes the divine action in this *indirect* form. This is true not just of the outer circumstances of action but also of the agent's internal cognitive and affective states. Further, God may also act *directly* to bring about various conditions of action. Miracles, in the sense of divinely caused events outside the ordinary course of nature, would be instances of such direct divine action. Not all direct acts of God in the world need be miracles, however. It may be, as I suggested above, that the world has an open structure, so that God can continuously act within it quite without disrupting its natural order.[24]

Now, it is important to notice that there will often be no need to specify which mode of divine action is at work in any instance. Consider, for example, a particular internal influence on action (say, a vivid recognition of the fellow humanity of a person in need or a glimpse of God's transcendent goodness through one of the mundane goods of life). I see no reason to decide whether such an effect is brought about by God (a) entirely through the causal structures of nature, or (b) through divine determination of natural indeterminacies, or (c) through direct action outside the order of probabilistic and/or causal regularities in nature. If we affirm that God acts to bring about this effect, we need only show that there is some possible way in which God might do so, and on this account there are several such possibilities. The key point is that basic Christian affirmations about God's agency in the creation and governance of the world entail that God is pervasively at work in establishing the external and internal context within which we act; God's agency envelopes and pervades our own.

Given theological incompatibilism, our free acts cannot be regarded

24. I develop this idea at greater length in "Particular Providence and the God of the Gaps," in *Chaos and Complexity: Scientific Perspectives on Divine Action*, ed. Robert John Russell, Nancey Murphy, and Arthur Peacocke (Vatican City: Vatican Observatory, 1994).

as direct acts of God[25] or as indirect divine acts determined by the history of the world God has made. But it should now be clear that God is uniquely situated to receive attributions of double agency in the third of the limited forms I noted above. Should we say, therefore, that (a) every free act of creatures can be regarded as God's act in a uniquely strong version of this type of double agency, and (b) all other events are either direct or indirect acts of God?

There are two reasons why this would claim too much. First, we cannot plausibly regard *all* of our free actions as God's own, for some of our actions are at odds with God's intentions for us. We can say that a free action is also or especially God's doing only when we also are prepared to affirm that whatever is distinctively good in that action reflects the workings of God's agency upon and within us. Second, if God is not a sufficient cause of our free acts, then neither is God a sufficient cause of the causal consequences of those acts. Free creaturely actions will initiate novel causal series in the world, and these will "infect" ever-expanding circles of events with this particular sort of causal contingency as a part of their ancestry. It will be true of all such events that they cannot entirely be attributed to God's agency. This entails, in particular, that the conditions under which I now act are shaped not only by God's agency but also by my own past free decisions and the free decisions of others. In granting the dangerous gift of freedom, God not only permits us to make self-determining choices but also allows us to live out the consequences of those choices. Insofar as those choices have been made badly, reflecting the varieties of ignorance and of evil, they will set the conditions for my future choices in ways that can be bad for me and (through my actions) for others. As a result, the capacity for free choice can be corrupted and distorted, so that our freedom itself comes to be in need of liberation. This is not a point that I will develop here, but it is worthy of mention, for it opens the way to the central issues of Christian soteriology.

There are, therefore, important respects in which the free acts of creatures can be regarded as God's acts. If we deny that God is the sufficient cause of the creature's free acts, we can immediately go on to affirm that God acts with the infinite resources of omnipotence to guide those choices by shaping the orienting conditions under which

25. This is not to deny, of course, that the agent and the agent's act would not exist if God did not directly sustain, or conserve, them. See note 15.

they are made. In untraceably many, varied, and subtle ways, God continuously brings to bear the pressure of the divine purpose for us without simply displacing our purposes for ourselves. God's action goes before our own, preparing us (in spite of ourselves) for the unsurpassably great good that God has promised us.[26]

26. For careful reading and comment on this essay I am indebted to David Cummiskey, Mark Okrent, and the members of the Theology Group. The essay benefited from discussion with colleagues at Hendrix College and at the 1991 Eastern Division meeting of the APA. Work on this project took place during the term of a fellowship from the National Endowment for the Humanities.

DIVINE ACTION AND HUMAN FREEDOM IN THE CONTEXT OF CREATION

David B. Burrell, C.S.C.

I am grateful for the opportunity to respond to Thomas Tracy's efforts to understand (and to correct) Kathryn Tanner's contention that a proper understanding of divine transcendence allows no incompatibility between creator and creatures being total causes in their respective domains, while creaturely causality is totally dependent upon the creator's. That Thomas Tracy would reach out to someone far more sympathetic to Kathryn Tanner's approach than to his signals his intellectual generosity. I hope to respond in the same largeness of spirit. While I am unable to comment on his presentation of Austin Farrer, I suspect that he overlooks an important polemical note in Farrer's demurral at *"explaining* the different senses in which and levels on which God and creatures act" (emphasis mine). Farrer hardly refused to "speculate about the metaphysics of [what he referred to as the paradox of] 'double agency'"; he rather eschewed attempting to explicate the *mechanics* of what he called the "causal joint" between infinite and finite action. That difference will prove crucial to our understanding Tracy's attempting "further explication of double agency," for such *explication* will not be the purported *explanation* that Farrer knew we had to avoid. And in this respect it seems that Tracy has profited from Farrer's animadversions. For what Farrer was after was a way of securing "the distinction" of God from the world, to use Sokolowski's controlling metaphor; or "the infinite qualitative difference," to gesture to Kierkegaard.[1] For the endemic tendency of philosophers treating divinity is to assign God a place in the universe, albeit the largest or the first or the most significant. Yet to say that "the distinction" is "glimpsed at the margin of reason, . . . at the intersection of reason and faith" (as Sokolowski does, 39) reminds us that the relation between God and creatures will not be easily explicated by categories tailored to the universe itself.

The title of Kathryn Tanner's major work, *God and Creation in Christian Theology,* should suggest that the "noncontrastive" view of God-in-relation-to-the-world will be secured only if we keep our focus on creation. That is, the God of whom we are speaking as Christians (and as Jews or Muslims as well) is the free creator of the universe. It is that description which guides the considerations of philosophical theology—as Aquinas puts it, "the beginning and end of all things and of reasoning creatures especially" (*ST* 1.2.Prol.)—and should also direct our metaphysical reflections on divine action. So "universal cause" will not mean *general* (as opposed to *particular*), but the all-pervasive cause-of-being, whose proper effect is the bestowal of *existing*, as the proper effect of the "universal" cause-of-all. (Such at least is Aquinas's reasoning: *ST* 1.45.5.) And our attempts to understand such a cause will require our assenting to an action that is not a change because it presupposes nothing and takes no time. So it will not be an action with which we are familiar, and if it can be said to be "the perfection of agency" (Tracy), it will be so in a way that not only involves "stripping away the limitations that attach to finite agents," but acknowledging that we are putting it to a use whose rules are quite unknown to us. While I agree with Tracy that this transcendent use "does not break down the basic logical structure of the

---

1. Robert Sokolowski, *The God of Faith and Reason* (Notre Dame, Ind.: University of Notre Dame Press, 1982), passim; and Søren Kierkegaard, *Concluding Unscientific Postscript,* passim.

concept [so that] we can coherently affirm *that* God is an agent [without being able] to spell out *what* it is to be such an agent," I would not conclude, as he does, that we are thus dealing with "a mode of agency that vastly exceeds our own." For that way of putting it also elides "the distinction," presuming that the "concept of *agency*" spans the "infinite qualitative difference" between creator and creatures on a continuum of degrees, with the creator "vastly exceeding" creatures.

That simply will not do, for the notions that can span "the distinction" do so only because they are able to function analogously, and as Tracy rightly remarks, we are able to assert them without *any* "mode of signification" whatsoever, to affirm the very *thing understood* of this One who is the source of all. And the reason we are able to do that reflects our faith that this One freely creates all that is, and so will leave "traces" of that activity in creation itself. Yet we will not be able to read off those traces as *divine*, like Friday's footprints. It is rather that the sign that they are divine traces rests with our recognition that all such "perfection terms" embody, in their ordinary use, an interior qualitative difference of the sort that Socrates recognized in acknowledging that he could indeed be said to be wise—provided we understood that the truly wise are those who recognize they are not wise. It is that interior qualitative difference that saves morality from being convention, while those who use evaluative language (like "agent") aware of its transcendent reaches will be hailed by ordinary people as "teaching with authority." The grammatical peculiarities of those terms in human language that also qualify as "names of God" seem to be accessible to most human beings, with little or no explicit reflection on their special semantic features. And we must keep them securely in mind as we try to negotiate the difficult territory that Austin Farrer found so formidable, reminding ourselves that "agent" as well as "cause" will always function analogously, and especially so when we attempt to articulate the relation of creature to creator. Yet the fact that we affirm that relation to be basic will also be able to guide our inquiry. In other words, "God's activity as creator" is far more than "a natural point at which to begin the discussion" of the "relation between divine and created agencies"; creation is the very paradigm for any and all divine activity that we know of, and bringing that awareness to our discussion will help ferret out misapprehensions of what Kathryn Tanner is saying. For Thomas Tracy's restatement of what she is saying makes a fatal transposition: if creatures "must be talked about as existing in a relation of total and immediate dependence upon God" (*God and*

Creation, 84), and "if God is said to found [created] causality or agency directly and *in toto*" (86), it does not follow that "God is always the total cause of each created event," as Tracy puts it.

The two factors crucial to an account of the creator-creature relation, both of which Tracy overlooks, are (1) that "divine providence works through intermediaries [with] God . . . from the abundance of divine goodness imparting to creatures also the dignity of causing" (*ST* 1.22.3), and (2) that the creator's primary effect is the *existence* of things. Nor are these two factors independent of each other, for God's bringing about the existence of both cause and effect in a cause-effect relationship means that each is brought to be *as* what it is, so that what exists as cause exercises its activity in such a way as to effect what results in the other. There is no need at all to conclude that the "only 'power and efficacy' exercised here is that which attaches to the divine agency." For the divine agency effects particular actions *through* the proper modality of creatures, as befits the creator, whose proper effect is the very *existing* of things. So Tracy is doubtless correct in demanding that Tanner's picturing the relationship as involving an intersection of vertical with horizontal planes be supplemented "to affirm the causal efficacy of creatures on the horizontal axis," but the required supplement is easily supplied by recalling that "God's activity on the vertical axis" is ever the activity of the creator: bestowing the very *existence* of things. The required mediating notion is that of *existing:* "this is how things receiving existence from God resemble [God]; for precisely as things possessing existence they resemble the primary and universal source of all existence" (*ST* 1.4.3). Yet "existing" is hardly a univocal term, such that creator and creatures might be seen as sharing in that general category, albeit antipodally.[2] And this, of course, is the sense in which Kathryn Tanner insists on a "noncontrastive understanding of transcendence."

"Contrast" is a patently ambiguous term, so the primary analogue operative in her exposition must be the notion of contraries within a genus: hence the key to our understanding the creator-creature relation—the "very specific one [relating the two agents] according to Christianity"— will have to be the reminder that *existence* is not a genus in which creator

---

2. Unless one insists on a characteristically "modern" reading of a metaphysics that attempts to display creation, whereby it will be presumed that "existence is an off/on property" (Christopher Hughes, *On a Complex Theory of a Simple God* [Ithaca, N.Y.: Cornell University Press, 1989], 27). But to do so would simply omit (and implicitly deny) what Tanner (with Aquinas) accepts as the guiding notion for explicating the metaphysics of these two agents.

and creatures share. As Aquinas puts it, in the context of explicating the "formal feature" of divine simpleness: "God is not even a prototype within the genus of substance, but the prototype of all being, transcending all genera" (*ST* 1.3.6.2); in short, God is not *a* being. And once the relevant "contrast" is presented in this fashion, "the very basic contrast at work in differentiating the causal roles of distinct agents" is hardly "problematic for theology," but a simple corollary to the fundamental theological and faith assertion of Jews, Christians, and Muslims: that the God in question is the free creator of the universe, whose action in creating presupposes nothing at all. More aggressively, there seems to be a dialectical relationship between our ability to think analogously of "agents" and our understanding of the creator-creature relationship. Theologies that attempt to circumvent this issue of creation, like those of the "process" variety, can think of God as exemplifying perfection categories preeminently, and so of God's agency as "the perfection of agency," but without any need to distinguish (as Tracy does) between the "manner of signifying" and the "thing signified."[3] Keeping one's intellectual focus on God as free creator assures that one not overlook the "infinite qualitative difference," and so have recourse to an analogical (rather than a "merely contrastive") characterization of divine attributes, and the ways in which the same expression might be used of creature and of creator. Alternatively, a univocal notion of *agent* in which none other than a freely originating creator can be said properly to be an agent, will staunchly maintain "the distinction," but at the price of created agency.[4] So it will not suffice simply to affirm the creator-creature relation as structuring the divine-human exchange; one will have to explicate it in a language supple enough to embody in use "the distinction" that creation requires.

If one does not do so, it seems that the result will inevitably take on the Mu'tazilite cast of Tracy's alternative proposals: that free human actions must be carried out in a space "independent" of the creator's activity, so that their "autonomy" can be assured. For the only alternative picture that Tracy can conjure up "whereby *everything* that creatures do is also done by God" is one in which "God establishes a universally

---

3. See my note, "Does Process Theology Rest on a Mistake?" *Theological Studies* 43 (1982): 125–35. The distinction is elaborated by Aquinas in treating "divine names" (*ST* 1.13.3).

4. This position fairly characterizes that of al-Ash'ari, which became the *sunna* of Islam: Daniel Gimaret, *Theories de l'acte humain en theologie musulmane* (Paris: Vrin, 1980).

deterministic order of created causes." But even if such a story were to be modified by a good dose of *chance*, it would hardly be compatible with the Jewish, Christian, or Muslim insistence that our response to the divine invitation be a free one. Yet, Tracy insists, even after we have corrected for the modal fallacy in arguments that contend that God's willing an event to occur entails that it occur necessarily, there remains a strictly theological problem with affirming that "God's willing that S choose to do A at t entails S choosing A at t," since the "key necessary condition for freedom . . . excludes determination not only by other created agents but also by the divine agent." But such a formulation simply presumes that God is like any other agent. What if God's willing something to take place were not to *entail* that event's occurring? And if the relation of creator to creation is not one of *entailment*, but a free bestowal of *existing* (with all its attendant perfections), would it not be natural to avoid the *entailment* relation when seeking a metaphysical explication of the relation between God's willing and created events? Granted that analogy alone will not do the trick, as Tracy notes in a further discussion of Farrer (in his note 19), but the kind of analogous discourse that is consonant with a creation ontology would seem to be called for.

Such discussions of human freedom, however, do seem doomed to present the divine-human encounter in "zero-sum" terms until we can begin to elaborate a richer conception of "creaturely freedom" than the current "libertarian" notion, which seems content with stating what Tracy recognizes to be "only the barest necessary condition for a strong conception of freedom." It is my contention that the required "strong conception" can be found in Aquinas's recasting of Aristotle's account of rational natures' inherent tending to an end, and the distinction that Aquinas stresses between "consent to the end" and "deliberation regarding the means," whereby *choosing* is relegated to the latter (and secondary) dimension of freedom and so ceases to present itself as the paradigm of free human activity. Yet that must be a story for another day. It is one more testimony to Tracy's awareness of alternative approaches to these questions that he underscores the inadequacy of the notion of freedom currently operative in these discussions. It is enough to say here, by way of commentary, that the final section of his paper, which sketches "useful analogical patterns for thinking about God's action in the actions of free creatures," will indeed prove useful for those who persist in thinking about God as another actor in the world. The fact that such a one is more a demiurge than a creator, however, should prove more than a little dissonant with "basic Christian [or Jewish or Muslim] affirmations about God's agency in the creation and governance of the world [which] entail that God is pervasively at work in establishing the external and internal context within which we act; [that] God's agency envelopes and pervades our own." For those affirmations certainly entail the total dependence of creatures on the creator on which Kathryn Tanner (with the majority tradition) insists, so what seems to be called for is a metaphysics capable of formulating that dependence in ways that respect all the modalities of creatures, including freedom. I have suggested, in my frequent allusions to Aquinas, that his metaphysics of *esse* (or *existing*) has the resources to do so, but commentators cannot be permitted to argue their points *in extenso*. As it is, I have prevailed altogether too much on Thomas Tracy's generous invitation.[5]

5. I have developed these points extensively and comparatively in *Freedom and Creation in Three Traditions* (Notre Dame, Ind.: University of Notre Dame Press, 1993).

CHAPTER 4

HUMAN FREEDOM, HUMAN SIN, AND GOD THE CREATOR

Kathryn E. Tanner

In this chapter I hope to clarify what a Christian belief in God as the creator of the world implies about human freedom and sin. The essay is a thought experiment: *if* one takes seriously the idea that God is the creator of all that is, what must one say about human freedom and human failing?

On the question of human freedom, I conclude that the idea of God as creator is compatible with *any* philosophical account of the nature of human freedom short of the theological judgment that human freedom requires freedom from or with respect to God. God's creative calling forth of the world does not conflict with human freedom, however one defines it. Whatever one's account of the natural and psychological conditions for human choice—however strongly one maintains the freedom of human choice from determination by psychological preconditions, natural circumstances, and so forth—human beings in the exercise of such freedom can still be considered the creatures of God, a part of what God's creative will for the world brings forth.

When thoughts turn to questions of human failing, here, I conclude, the idea of God the creator sets its own limits on intelligibility. The origination of sin is properly a mystery, properly inexplicable in a scheme of thought where God is the ultimate principle of explanation. Human beings must be the ones responsible for their own moral failing since God by definition brings to be only the good; but the *how* of that human-originated sin is as Karl Barth says an impossible possibility, the surd of a creature turning against its own being given by God, as Bernard Lonergan avers, an inconceivable breaking off of the very relation to God that makes the creature all that it is. What power or act could that turning against or that breaking off be when all that one is comes from God and all that comes from God is good?

Neither question of human freedom or human failing as I have posed it will appear to have much force—and therefore the conclusions will not seem to matter very much—without some sense of what I mean by serious consideration of belief in God as the creator of the world. It is this belief in its extremity, in its almost wild implications when taken seriously, when ridden consistently through to its logical end, that makes the question of human freedom and sin in a world that God creates interesting.

The claim that God is the creator of the world is a distinguishing affirmation of the Christian tradition: one would be hard-pressed to maintain one's identity as a Christian without it. In a certain strand of the Christian theological tradition, however, this claim is made the abiding presupposition for all discussion of God's relation to the world; for example, in discussing God's providential guiding of human affairs, forgiveness of sins and elevation of human beings to glory in Christ, gifts of grace and so forth.[1] In a narrow sense God is the creator as the giver of existence, where the fact of being is contrasted with what one is or does or becomes. But in a broader sense, God acts in the mode of creator whatever the aspect of created existence at issue: existing, acting, relating to others, finding a new life in Christ. From the most general to the most specific features of existence, all that the creature

---

1. In *God and Creation in Christian Theology* (Oxford: Basil Blackwell, 1988) I argue that this is a quite pervasive strand of the Christian theological tradition, spanning a number of historical periods, theological schools, and denominational affiliations.

is it owes to God as the creator of the world. This is a vision of a God supremely beneficent, a giver of gifts beyond any human giver's capacities to comprehend, to whom it is fitting to raise one's voice in joyful thanksgiving and without whom, it is appropriate to confess in utmost humility, one is literally nothing.[2]

What does it mean to take the claim that God is the creator of the world this seriously? What does it mean to push the implications of such a claim this far?

One can say, first of all, that God's creation of the world loses any specific reference to a beginning time or initiating moment: to be created is to be in a relation of dependence upon God that holds whenever and for however long one exists. This relation of dependence upon God is absolute, moreover, in three distinct senses—in its range, manner, and efficacy.

The relation must be said to be all inclusive or universally extensive: everything nondivine, in every respect that it is, is dependent upon God's creative activity, which brings it forth. God's creative activity calls forth or holds up into being throughout the time of its existence what has its own integrity as a nondivine existence, and this nondivine existence has to be considered the consequence of God's creative calling forth and holding up *as a whole*, in its order and in its entirety, in every detail and aspect. Nondivine existence maintained by God's creative power constitutes, therefore, a *whole plane or level* of nondivine existence, inclusive of every item or order that is or happens or becomes in the world as we know it. Such a claim of universal scope holds, it is important to note, insofar as existence and its aspects are good. Existence and goodness are convertible according to this account, since God is by definition a supremely good God who brings forth, therefore, only the good as creator.

This relation of dependence upon God is, furthermore, always and in every respect a *direct* or immediate relation of dependence upon God. Picture the plane of nondivine existence (which is the whole of the world as we know it) suspended in existence at each and every one of its points, and therefore in its entirety, by God's creative action. In such a picture every nondivine being in every respect owes all that it is directly to God *whatever* its relations with other nondivine beings,

---

2. Which of these two attitudes—thanksgiving or humility—a theologian emphasizes depends upon his or her theological priorities and the perceived needs of a particular situation.

the specific natures of those relations, their presence or absence, etc. The relation of dependence upon God, which suspends any and every nondivine being or aspect of being into existence, is not affected by the relations (causal, temporal, spatial, etc.) among nondivine beings, by relations *within* the plane of nondivine existence. God does not call forth or hold up into being any creature as the existing, acting, interacting being it is *by way of* other creatures, by way of their existence, actions, or interactions with it. Actions, mutual influences, causal relations, and so forth among the nondivine may be a part of the world God calls forth, but they are the *results* of God's creative action (if it is indeed universal in scope) and not the *conditions or means* of that creative calling forth.

Because all that is nondivine is the consequence and not the condition of God's creative calling forth or holding up, one should say, finally, that God's creative intention for the world cannot be hindered, diverted or otherwise redirected by creatures. Lacking any defect or internal principle of corruption, moreover, God's creative calling forth is indeed unconditionally and necessarily efficacious. Expressing the idea in the oft-used terms of "willing" and "intending," a theologian of our ilk asserts that what God wills for the world as its creator must happen in just the way God wills. The point of such an assertion is not at bottom to stress God's irrepressible or tyrannical *control*—although something close to that may sometimes be pertinent as a rhetorical device to meet the needs of a particular audience, say, to pull up short those who thanklessly elevate themselves to an existence independent of God. The point is the same as always: to make clear the implications of God's supreme beneficence as creator. Such an assertion is a simple consequence of the other conclusions we have drawn from that beneficence: God creates immediately, without any process in which creatures might figure, so there is nothing to get in the way; God creates without any exception so there is nothing besides the effects of God's own creative calling forth to complicate it.[3]

Human Freedom under God

What does this account, or picture, of God the creator imply about human freedom under God? Theologians who assume the above picture or ac-

3. See my *God and Creation* for a fuller exposition and defence of this picture.

count will want to say that any power or free action attributed to human beings exists in an absolute relation of dependence upon God. According to the account given above it makes no sense to claim that human beings have attributes that are good but that are not dependent upon God in that way: this would just be to say that human beings in those respects are not created. The premise that all nondivine beings exist in an absolute relation of dependence upon God would have in that case an exception.

Theologians holding the picture of God the creator I have outlined would be especially reluctant to make such an exception of human power and free action since what is at stake here is a proper recognition of God's beneficence. All that we have for good we have received from God. The more valuable the attribute of free agency the more the concern to claim that it is a created gift. The greater the good of free choice the greater the love for God that is appropriate. The greater the good the greater the need for humility, for thankfulness in recognition that one has received from God even that of which one is most proud.

Any attempt to exempt human powers from an absolute relation of dependence upon God can only be suspected, from this point of view, of Titanism. What is it that motivates the desire to exempt the greatest attributes of a specifically human existence from dependence upon God, if not the desire to be unbeholden to God in some way for the greatness of what one is? In the most important respects one would be able to say that one is not God's creature. (Or perhaps that one *is* a creature of God in those respects but at some remove that lessens one's dependence upon God's gracious giving.)[4]

4. The theologian inclined to exempt human agency from the sort of relation of dependence upon God I have specified will have, of course, his or her own reasons for doing so: for example, in order to render sin more easily explicable, in order to stress human responsibility for good and evil and therefore encourage moral striving, in order to protect God's justice. The theologian holding the picture of God the creator I have outlined can respond that some of these concerns (e.g., the concern for human responsibility) can finally be assured just as well without the exception of human agency from an absolute relation of dependence upon God. (I shall in fact be arguing this later.) Or, the theologian can claim that some concerns (e.g., the concern to protect God's justice) are served no better with such an exception. (If God has the simple power to prevent or block the harmful consequences of human sin, the independence of human agency from God's creative working hardly lessens God's responsibility for the suffering of innocents brought about by human malfeasance.) Finally, our theologian can admit that some of these concerns (e.g., concern for the intelligibility of sin) may in fact be better addressed by exempting human agency from an absolute relation of dependence upon God. This advance just comes, the theologian can argue, at too great a price. Sin may be more easily explicable when human acts are not thought to be called forth by a good God, but the same sort of account of meritorious human acts suggests that human beings in some essential respect save themselves. Fundamental differences of theological priority are what ultimately distinguish,

Although the theologians holding the picture of God as creator I have been talking about may not *want* to exempt human agents from an absolute relation of dependence upon God, it is another question whether there can *be* any free human agency when God's agency is understood that way. Should free human agency exist, it must exist in an absolute relation of dependence upon God if the premises about creation that we have been looking at are assumed. But this does not say anything about whether any notion of human freedom worth its salt is compatible with that relation to God to begin with. Exactly what sort of power or freedom can be attributed to human beings if one assumes the picture of creation sketched above? At what point, if any, will the attribution of freedom and power to human beings conflict with that account?

There are two possible sources of conflict. The characteristic shape of human action may be incompatible with the very notion of an absolute relation to God as creator that we have outlined. Or, the character of human action may not obviously conflict with that notion but with its implication, God's sovereignty as we have expressed it, the infallible efficacy of God's calling forth, which was predicated on the idea that no creature's power of influence extends to God's creative working.

To explore these two possible sources of conflict, the characteristics of human action at issue have to be specified and considered separately. We shall first consider human agency at its bare minimum, as a power to bring about effects within the world, human agency considered, that is, under the generic notion of a cause of effects. Then we shall look at human action as a specifically human form of free agency, dividing the notion of freedom into two—freedom in the sense of having one's choices in one's own power, and in the sense of freedom of choice. There are many different notions of human freedom in the Western philosophical tradition; the ones I discuss are chosen to maximize the possibility of conflict with our picture of God as creator.[5] If such conflicts are avoidable, presumably conflicts with *any* account of human freedom are avoidable.

Should conflicts with our picture of God the creator arise on any of

---

therefore, theologians who are from those who are not willing to exempt human agency from an absolute relation of dependence upon God.

5. E.g., they are accounts of human freedom from a libertarian rather than a compatibilist point of view. If human freedom is generally consistent with determinism, as compatibilists hold, the existence of a God who creates according to our picture is unlikely to pose any additional problems.

these scores, the theologian holding onto that picture has several options: (1) deny that human power or freedom has to be characterized in that way in order to be genuine; (2) agree that human power or freedom must be of that sort to be worthy of the name and accept the consequence that human beings do not have any; (3) permit such characterizations but limit their scope so that they appropriately hold for relations *within* the created plane of existence but not for the creature's relation of dependence upon God. This restriction on its sphere of applicability, the theologian insists, does nothing to take away from any genuine sense of human power or freedom.[6] This third option is the one we shall follow.

Let us begin with the question of human power to effect things within the world, a power we would like to attribute, presumably, to any number of created beings, animate and inanimate, human or nonhuman. Can a creature have genuine power *of its own* if that power exists in virtue of an absolute relation of dependence upon God? Can a power of creatures to bring about effects within the created order or plane of existence be real if it is received from God, brought about by God's creative calling forth?

The response to this line of questioning is implicit in the account of God as creator we have already outlined. If it makes sense to say that God can call forth a nondivine being with an integrity of existence of its own, then it makes sense to say that God can call forth nondivine beings with real powers of their own to influence other creatures. The cases are exactly parallel according to the picture of God as creator I have outlined. God creatively evokes not just the fact that the creature exists (in a narrow sense) but the existing of the creature as all that it is—including powers of operation on its part. The powers of creatures would just be a part, therefore, of the whole plane of nondivine existence that God calls forth and suspends in being. According to our picture, a creature can have a real power to bring about effects in the created order but without God's holding in being of that creature and its capacities, such powers are nothing.

Someone disputing the possibility that genuine powers are part of a God-given plane of nondivine existence has the burden of proving *either* that the idea of God the creator is incoherent altogether—incoherent

---

6. Insofar as he or she is simply an upholder of the picture of God the creator we have outlined, the theologian need not form any judgment on the matter of whether a libertarian account, say, is the proper way to describe the human power or freedom that is exercised within and with respect to the nondivine plane of existence.

where existence (in a narrow sense) is the putative result of God's creative working as well as where created powers are—*or* that something about the idea of creatures with real power simply prevents an otherwise coherent account of God the creator of all from being extended specifically to it. The former option threatens to push the theologian out of a Christian orbit. The second option is just that—an option, a possibility without material force—until actual arguments are supplied.

One such argument might be that created powers cannot be real if, as we have implied above, God as the creator of all directly brings about the created effects that the exercise of those created powers are themselves supposed to produce. If God on God's own is bringing about the effect in those respects, then the creature is not exercising any real power; it is just going through the motions. If the creature's own operations are to make any real contributions to the effect produced, then God's creative working must be superfluous to just that extent. God's creative working simply should not be said to extend, therefore, to what creatures themselves produce.

This argument operates, however, with a fundamentally different picture of God's creative working than the one we started with, and so fails to prove what it sets out to prove. This argument does not, as billed, assume our picture of God's creative working and show the impossibility of its covering the specific case of nondivine powers. Its fundamental premises about God's creative working are simply not ours. This argument does not think of God's creative action as what holds up into existence a whole nondivine plane of being but assumes from the start, without argument, that God is one actor among other possible actors within a single plane of cooperating and/or competing causes of a comparable sort. Only on that assumption would it make sense to think that God's bringing about of a created effect must render superfluous a creature's own bringing about of that effect, and vice versa.

According to our picture, if a creature exercises any power at all, it does so on a different plane or axis, so to speak, from that along which God's creative agency is exercised. God works to hold the whole of that created plane in existence and does not work within it. If a nondivine cause works to produce an effect, it does so only insofar as it is held up into existence in those respects by God. No matter how genuine the creature's power, that does not render superfluous, therefore, God's own working.

The same sort of defect affects the other side of the argument—the crucial side for the question at hand, the question whether, given our account of God's creative working, creatures can have any real power at all. The argument of our opponent pictures God bringing about a created effect, not by suspending into existence that created effect along with everything else, but by some sort of special, individual activity of God himself within the created order that brings God into possible competition with a creature's own actions for that effect. God's working as creator renders the idea of the creature's own working otiose, as our opponents argue, only when God's direct calling forth of the effect of that creature's action is considered in isolation from all the rest of what God as creator calls forth, as if God brings about that effect directly and not also and equally directly any creature acting within the plane of nondivine existence to bring it about, and therefore as if God were to bring about that created effect by some other act than the creative act by which God holds up into existence the whole plane of nondivine being. None of these assumptions comport with our original picture of God's creative working. They are not, moreover, conclusions drawn from that picture's critique, but unexamined premises. Why must we accept them?

Let us suppose we have answered satisfactorily questions about the compatibility of nondivine power with the idea of creatures existing in an absolute relation of dependence upon God. At the least, there are no obvious grounds for conflict. The conclusions about God's sovereignty that we drew from our picture of God as creator might still supply other grounds for thinking that the genuine power of creatures presents problems. Let us try to resolve possible conflicts on these grounds now.

It would surely seem, first of all, that a creature's powers could be genuine even if it is a part of our account of God's sovereignty that such powers are not exercised with respect to God. It would be enough for those powers to operate with respect to things within the created order, that is, to have a range of exercise within the plane of nondivine reality. Such a range of exercise would not imply power with respect to God and therefore conflict with our claims for God's sovereignty, since, according to our account of God's creative action, the creature's powers to make things happen within the world are always the result of God's creative working and never its condition. If this is the reason creatures lack power vis-à-vis God, such a lack of power would not vitiate human power with respect to creatures. On the contrary, a lack of power vis-à-vis God is a *precondition* for it: the creature's absolute relation of dependence upon God is what brings it about that the creature has any of the powers it does.

Claims for the power of human beings within the created order need not conflict, then, with the *efficacy* of God's creative working as we have presented it. Created causes, if they exist, are simply a part of what God calls forth as creator; as the result of God's creative working rather than its condition, the powers of creatures are not in any position to stand in the way of what God wants to create. To the extent God intends to bring forth a world in which things happen by way of created causes, those causes, far from being in potential conflict with the efficacy of God's will, are its executors. Though not the means by which God holds up into being a world of causally related beings, such causes are bringing about along the plane of nondivine existence just the sort of world God is working to suspend into being.

The *manner in which* the efficacy of God's creative working is assured on our account, moreover, does not conflict with the dignity or integrity of human power. The infallibility of God's creative working need not take away from the power of creatures or the efficacy of such powers, should they exist. God does not have to do without a world in which creatures have their own power in order for God's creative working to be infallibly efficacious. It is the universal scope of God's creative working—its reference to the powers and operations of creatures as well as everything else, that makes it so. Indeed, far from being incompatible with God's power, God's gift of power to creatures is a clearer indication of the greatness of God's power, of its might, one could say, than the withholding of that gift: the supremacy of the giver is measured by the gifts.

In virtue of the same universality of scope we just mentioned, the infallibility of God's creative working need not be ensured, either, by *hindering* the operations of created beings, thereby conflicting with the dignity of their status as genuine causes. God *could* get God's way, so to speak, by a general policy of blocking the operations of created causes whenever they run contrary to what God wills. But according to our picture of God as creator there is no need for this recourse. Without jeopardizing God's infallible efficacy, human beings can retain a kind of Lockean freedom "to do whatever they choose to do"; they can in fact execute what they intend. Like other created causes of effects within the world, human beings are generally able to operate and effect those things within the created order that accord with their own powers of operation.

Let us turn now to the distinguishing features of human action and leave behind these generic aspects of action shared with other sorts of created causes. There are two distinct clusters of notions specifying the sort of powers one would like to claim for human beings. Questions about the compatibility of human powers with the account of God and creation I have given tend to focus around these two ideas.

The first cluster of notions concerns what might be called freedom of spontaneity or freedom of self-origination, terms that indicate the voluntary character of human choosing and the freedom of human beings to move themselves to choose. Choice is within our power; we have power over our choices—that is what is at issue here.

This kind of claim is understood in a number of different ways in the history of speculation on the topic. It means at least some of the following to some people: (1) If one moves oneself to choose, that choice follows of necessity; that is, that choice *has* to come about. My will is always in my power in the sense that the immediate efficacy of moving myself to choose cannot be impeded. (2) Choice is in my power in the sense that I choose to do only what I want to do. My choosing is always a matter of my own inclination, my own tending. (3) My choosing is therefore always voluntary. I cannot be brought to choose something against my will. I can be made to *do* something against my will but I cannot be forced to *choose* to do that against my will. Threat of harm, for example, can make me choose to do what, all things being equal, I would rather not, but I still make the choice in such circumstances for what I view to be a greater good. (For example, I choose to cooperate with my captors because that seems better than being killed for my resistance.) (4) Power over my choosing, if it exists at all, cannot be alienated. Human beings cannot be brought to choose *apart from their own choosing*; no one can choose *for me*. (5) The determination of choice and its specifications end with the human agent in the sense that none of the following factors constrains or necessitates a particular choice: (a) the natural and situationally determined constitution of a human agent (its natural inclinations, transient feelings, bodily state) does not determine choice, although it does make certain objects of choice desirable. Human beings retain power over their choices insofar as they retain the capacity to assess whether, say, such desires are good ones to have or appropriate to act upon in the particular circumstances. Some assessment of this sort is at work where, say, my hunger makes my neighbor's food desirable but I do not choose to take it since that would involve an act of theft. (b) The *objects of choice* that a situation presents do not constrain choice for the same reason. Finding, for example, $100,000 in unmarked bills does not constrain my choice to keep and spend them. None of this is to say that passions, physical torture, and so forth, cannot necessitate choice by distracting one from due consideration or by literally driving one out of one's mind in a way that precludes rational assessment of desires and available objects of choice. It is just to say that in those instances one has *lost* power over one's choices. (c) The rational assessment of the greater good in a particular situation does not necessitate one's choosing it. Unless that proposed object of choice is apprehended as good in every conceivable respect, human beings retain the power to choose neither the greater nor the lesser good. (The will, in other words, has the power not to choose between them at all.) One can also move for the *reassessment* of what has been perceived to be the greater good, under some other aspect. (For example, it may be better to burn cheap oil than invest in solar energy if one considers immediate expenditures, but one might also go on to consider the prospects for environmental damage.)

These last considerations of freedom from constraint lead to a second cluster of notions regarding human agency, about which we can be much briefer. Human beings are free insofar as they have *free choice:* the freedom to choose to do something or not, and the freedom to choose one thing or another.

Let us begin our discussion of possible conflicts with our picture of God as creator by looking at the first cluster of notions. (We will assume here the goodness of the human agent and its choices.) Are any of these notions of freedom of spontaneity or self-origination incompatible with a human agent's absolute relation of dependence upon God? In other words, do my choices remain within my own power in the senses specified if these very choices exist in virtue of God's creative action for them?

Would, for example, the necessity with which my choice follows upon my moving myself so to choose (that is, the immediate efficacy of the will for its own choice) lessen the dependence of that choice upon God's creative working for it, and therefore conflict with our premises regarding creation? No: the dependence of my choice upon my moving myself so to choose does not have any such effect since, according to our premises, God's creative calling forth must be directly behind the choice *and* my moving myself so to choose *and* the character of the relation between the two as one of necessary consequence. The dependence of my choice upon God's calling it forth is not affected in any way—it is not lessened (or strengthened)—by the fact my choice is dependent upon my moving myself so to choose within the created plane of existence, since that whole plane of existence is held in being by God.

Would not the necessary efficacy of my moving myself to choose conflict, however, with the *freedom* of God's creative intention for the world? Given the necessary efficacy of my moving myself to choose, would not God's creative calling forth of my moving myself to choose constrain God to call forth that *choice* as well? No: according to our picture of God as creator, if my moving myself to choose has a necessary efficacy, God has simply called forth a world in which choices necessarily follow upon human beings moving themselves to choose. According to our picture, God does not first call forth my moving myself to choose and then, because of that fact, creatively call forth those choices that must follow upon my so moving given its necessary efficacy. God's creative calling forth, in a single act so to speak, simply holds up into being the whole of the world in which human beings' moving themselves to choose has a necessary efficacy.

In general, necessary relations between created causes and effects do not conflict with the freedom of God's creative intention. If God's creative calling forth is free and not necessitated, God does not have to bring about a world in which such necessary relations occur to begin with. Even if the sort of power over choices that we have been talking about is part of what it *means* to be human, so that God could not choose to create *human* beings without granting them that power, God still retains the freedom to choose to create such beings or not. Given the existence of such beings, and that means given the fact of God's will for them, the necessity with which a particular choice follows upon my moving my will to choose it does not make that choice (absolutely) necessary in any way that would require that such a choice be a part of God's creative intention for the world. That choice necessarily follows upon my so moving myself, but only insofar as I exist long enough in so moving myself to effect my choice.[7] In other words, my necessity of efficacy assumes the existence of myself moving. If a part of what God calls forth is a world in which my existence in the process of self-moving terminates before being efficacious, the necessary efficacy that characterizes my self-moving becomes a moot point—such a choice will not occur.

As a matter of fact, human beings do not generally suffer this sort of annihilation in the process of choosing. According to our premises, this

---

7. We have been assuming all along that one's moving oneself to choose and the choice itself are really distinct, a process and its term, and therefore that the necessary efficacy of the former is not the result of any immediate identity between the two.

fact does not indicate that God *could not* call forth a world of that sort. It is simply an indication that, in keeping with our picture of God as a gracious giver, God's actual creative intention includes a respect for the integrity of human operations.

Even if these arguments convince, a critic might charge that the *rest* of what freedom of spontaneity or self-origination implies conflicts with God's creative calling forth of human agency. For example: (1) If God brings me to choose, the choice is no longer a matter of my own choosing. (2) If God brings me to choose, God can make me choose against my will. That is, God can do violence to my will by making me choose what I am not inclined myself to choose. (More strongly, God can make me choose what I am inclined *not* to choose.) (3) If God brings me to choose, I do not choose but God chooses for me.

A theologian holding our picture of God as creator has the same basic response (with minor variations) to this cluster of charges. Taking each charge in turn, he or she can say: (1) If God creatively calls forth someone's choosing, God's creative action is not *replacing* that human being's choosing. Indeed, the human agent itself choosing is what God holds up into being. God's calling forth of the human being's choosing does not alienate the human being's power to choose. On the contrary, according to our picture it brings it about as something that is the human being's own. (2) Since according to our premises God's creative calling forth extends to the whole of what happens, it is a mistake to isolate a human being's *choice* as what God brings about so as to suggest that God is not also bringing about the human agent in its very moving of itself so to choose. When God brings about a human being in its choosing, the choice remains, therefore, a matter of the human being's own inclinations so to choose. (3) If human choosing is always dependent in this way upon God's will for it, it no longer makes sense to talk about God forcing someone to choose what he or she would otherwise not choose. The creature *has* no inclinations to choose except for the ones God gives. The human being may have had inclinations to the contrary a moment before, but given God's calling forth of a change in them, the creature has just those inclinations, which God intends, in the next moment, and no others.

One final possibility of conflict remains within this cluster of notions concerning human freedom of spontaneity or self-origination. Can choice end with the human agent (in the sense that a human being is not constrained to choose or to choose one thing rather than another by its own physical constitution, apprehended objects or evaluative judgments) if human choosing exists in an absolute relation of dependence upon God? A suspicion that it cannot may be based on an argument that God's calling forth of that choosing could not be *infallible* (as we have said) without some constraints of those sorts. How can God's calling forth of a human agent's choice be infallible, if the human being's so choosing is not necessitated by any created conditions?

The theologian holding to our picture can answer that the infallibility of God's creative working would require human choosing to be necessitated by created conditions only if God's creative working were not *itself* directly efficacious of that result. If God's creative working brought a person to make a particular choice *by way of* certain created conditions— by way of his/her situation or physical states or thoughts of desirable courses of action—then indeed, God's creative calling forth of that person's choice would be infallibly effective only if those created conditions were. According to our premises, however, God's creative intention is directly behind both the choosing and the created influences on it. God's will for a person's choice remains direct and directly efficacious, therefore, irrespective of the existence of created influences for such a choice. The human being's choosing in the way he or she does *has* to come about simply because God's creative working extends to a choice of that sort, and not because created conditions *constrain* such a choice.

The critic of our picture will no doubt charge that it is just *God's creative working* that is the problem. One problem might be this: even if the necessary infallibility of God's working does not require other created causes to necessitate the human agent's choice, choice does not end with the human agent. *God* brings the human agent to choose and therefore a human being cannot be the agent-cause of its own choice.

One can respond to this objection in two ways. First, God does not bring about the human agent's choice by intervening in the created order as some sort of supernatural cause, so as to make up the difference between created conditions and the human being's choice and to supply that otherwise missing factor or impetus that takes away the indifference of the human will and brings about choice in a particular direction. God simply brings about, by that selfsame act of holding up into existence, the whole of a world in which human choices occur *without* any sufficient causes for them within the happenings of the world. If a picture of divine intervention is behind the idea that choice does not end with the human agent but is necessitated by the influence of God, then such a conclusion is mistaken.

Second, choice ends with the human agent within the plane of non-divine existence, even if God is the creator of that world, and it is with reference to that nondivine plane that the idea of choice ending with the human agent was originally defined. If God is the creator of the world, one can still affirm a very strong libertarian version of the human being's freedom from constraint by physical impulse, situation, apprehended goods, and so forth. A theologian holding to our picture will argue that that is enough to make the idea of agent-causation meaningful. If the critic insists that human choice can genuinely end with the human agent only if *God* is not also bringing about the agent choosing, is that not finally to push a theological claim? One insists that the nonnecessitated character of human choice be taken so far that human beings are no longer creatures.

If the claim that human choice is not necessitated by any given conditions must be taken in an absolute sense, with a universal reference that includes God's creative working among those conditions, then the theologian can only say that such a thing does not exist. In defense, he or she can say, however, that the conditions failing to necessitate choice may include anything and everything *short* of God's will; he or she is merely insisting on theological grounds that the human being is still the creature of God.

It makes sense according to our picture of God as creator to restrict in this way the sort of conditions relevant for determining whether choices end with the human agent—to restrict them to created conditions—since God according to that picture is not positioned along with the created conditions of choice and human agents within a single plane or arena of cause-effect operations. As we have said before, God is not a factor among factors that are together sufficient to bring about human choices; God is instead the one who brings to be the whole of the created order in all its aspects where some happenings are necessitated by others and some (a person's choices) are not.

A second objection to God's bringing about of a human being's choices would be that God's infallible working *necessitates* human choice even if no created happenings do. The human being cannot choose to do other than as God intends. This brings us to the second cluster of notions of human freedom: the freedom to choose or not to choose, to choose one thing or another. If God's creative working for a particular person's choice is infallible, then that person must choose and choose as God wants that person to choose. Human beings cannot be said, therefore, to have freedom of choice.

A theologian holding our picture cannot deny that, given God's infallible working, human beings *must* choose when and what God wills. This theologian can simply try to take away from the critic the senses of this "must" that make it objectionable.

First, he or she can argue that, if one limits the relevant conditions for a determination of free choice to *created* conditions, this "must" does not mean that a human agent loses freedom of choice. Even if a human being must choose what God wants him or her to choose, there may be nothing about the physical constitution of this human agent or what has happened in the world up until now or the laws of nature or the desirability of available objects of choice or any other created condition of choice, in any combination, that necessitates a choice or a choice of any particular sort by that agent. The same arguments we considered on the question of agent-causation return here.

Second, if the human being's *capacity* to do otherwise is understood in terms of this failure of any combination of given created causes to constrain choice, one can meaningfully say that a human being is *able* (given the same created conditions) to choose otherwise than the agent does, even if the agent never chooses anything other than what God wills that agent to choose.

It is true that if the necessary infallibility that characterizes God's calling forth of a human choice were to necessitate that choice *absolutely*, it would not be possible to say that the creature has the ability to choose otherwise vis-à-vis the created conditions of choice. A theologian holding to our picture has to deny that the necessity with which a human being's choice follows from God's will for it makes that choice simply and in all respects necessary. It is usual to appeal here to an analogy with modal operators of logical necessity. "If q follows necessarily from p, then q is necessary" is a false proposition of modal logic, where p is "God's calling forth of a human choice" (or will that a human choice occur) and q is "that human choice occurs." If p were necessary then q would be too but, on our premises, p is not necessary (God does not *have* to create anything).[8]

8. The necessity of immutability of God's creative will for q on the supposition God does so will (i.e., the fact that given such a will for q it cannot be changed) is also not enough to make q itself necessary, unless in analogous cases (e.g., p is a statement about the past) one is willing to say the same. I do not think one *should* be so willing for cases of past fact. If, for example,

What then does the inability of a human agent to do otherwise than God wills *mean* if the human agent's choice is not necessitated by any created conditions? A theologian who holds to our picture of God as creator might claim that this is an inability like that whereby I say that insofar as I *am* choosing to do something I cannot choose *not* to so choose. This inability to do otherwise would be like the creature's inability to do other than what *God* wills in that it would hold even under the most libertarian of circumstances. All it means is that I cannot choose and not choose to do the same thing at the same time. If I *am* choosing to do it at T, I *cannot* choose *not to* at T. But this sort of inability does not indicate any real inability not to choose at T what I *do* choose. If the analogy holds, I am not free to choose to do anything at T other than what God wills that I choose to do at T, but this also says nothing about any real inability of mine at T to do something else.

Whether or not, however, one accepts the conclusion of this argument that human beings have a real ability to do otherwise, this analogy suggests that my choosing as God wills me to choose follows with the same necessity as my choosing as I do when I am so choosing; and that is a very strong necessity indeed. I may have a real ability to do otherwise in a certain situation, but given God's will for my making a particular choice that ability is not exercised: I make that choice and no other. In a similar sense, my real ability to choose A is not (and in the sense specified above cannot be) exercised in case I actually choose B. We may have the real ability at T to choose in a way that diverges from the choice God wills that we make at T, but, given the will of God, we never actually choose anything but what God wills us to choose; what's more, if the argument we made regarding our first cluster of notions about human freedom holds, we never *want* to choose anything else.

---

at T_1 in Athens Socrates' running necessitates Socrates' moving, the fact that Socrates' running at that time in Athens is a matter of past fact at T_2 and so cannot be changed (it has a kind of necessity of immutability), does not make Socrates' moving at T_1 any *more* necessary than it was at T_1. It was at T_1, and in retrospect remains at T_2, a contingent matter of fact.

A critic could also claim that the original analogy with modal operators of necessity is no good: the necessity with which a human person's choice follows from God's will for it is not a mere logical necessity but some sort of causal necessity. I fail to see, however, how that changes the falsity of the relevant modal formula. Again, to take a more ordinary example: "If I move myself to choose to do something, it follows of necessity that I choose to do it." This necessity of consequence is based upon the necessity of efficacy by which one brings about one's own choice. No one would conclude, I think, from this relation of necessity that a particular choice is itself necessary and that freedom of choice with respect to it is thereby eliminated.

Is this sort of freedom of choice under God a freedom of choice worthy of the name? Whatever the case, I believe it is the only sense of human freedom of choice compatible with a consistent application of the notion of creation we are working with. Were one to *drop* the attribution of freedom of choice to human beings, it is not clear in this era of Frankfurt cases what exactly would be lost. Human beings would still remain *responsible* for the choices they make (the good ones at least, since that is all we have been talking about so far), in virtue of the fact that the first cluster of notions regarding human freedom would still hold: human beings would remain the agent-causes of choices they make willingly.

Human Sin under God

Christians affirm the existence of human sin, however, and this would seem to suggest that human beings *are* able *not* to choose what God wills them to choose, in a stronger sense than we have admitted so far. It would seem that the human being who sins *actually chooses* other than God wills. If God is good, God's will is never for the sinful aspects of human life per se, and therefore the existence of sin must run contrary in fact to God's creative intentions for the world. Given the existence of sin, human freedom of choice must include the freedom to make a choice that is contrary to the choice God wills a person to make.

It would seem, then, that a theologian who holds our picture of God as creator and who acknowledges the existence of sin should follow through on the implications of this sort of freedom to sin, and admit: (1) Sinful choices present an exception to our premises about creation. Some aspect of nondivine being exists without being in an absolute relation of dependence upon God's will for it. (2) Human beings in making sinful choices exercise a freedom from God. (3) God's creative will for the world cannot, therefore, be infallible of itself with respect to anything that happens in the world that is influenced by the sinful choices human beings make.

The familiar response to the first objection is to say that sin is essentially a defect, a lack, something missing. Sin does not exist per se but as a defect "exists," parasitic upon what does exist, an absence with a horrible enough sort of presence insofar as what is missing is essential or proper to what does exist. Because sin is not an "existing" aspect of created being, God's creative will should not extend to it on our premises: it is not therefore an exception to them. As a lack parasitic upon what is, sin does, however, remain in a sense absolutely dependent upon God, for without the created being that a defect affects, a defect would not be a defect but absolutely nothing, and *that* created being *is* in the usual absolute relation of dependence upon God.

Assuming the adequacy of this response, the hard part, however, is to account for how a sinful defect comes about without God's direct creative will for the activity of whatever it is that brings it about. Such activity, insofar as it is itself something, must be called forth by God in its operation and efficacy or our premise about God as a creator would be violated. If God does so, God directly effects the created activity that brings about sin, stopping short only of the defect of sin itself, which is small comfort. One might try to say that the activity that brings about the defect of sin does so in virtue of its own defect and that God does not directly will the activity in that respect. But this simply pushes the question of the origin of sin back to the question of what brought about the first defect. The question has to stop somewhere since, according to our premises, God does not create a world of sin. But wherever one stops, God's will would seem to be behind whatever created activity brings sin about.

Perhaps the defect of sin is not the result of a creature's action but of its *inaction*. The defect of sin is not brought about by any real *activity*, in the way a defect in a work of art might come about by taking a sledge-hammer to it, but simply by a failure (the way, say, the gears of a mechanism might fail to catch, sending everyone on a ski lift plummeting to their deaths). The human being does not take into account everything that needs to be taken into account in order to make a proper judgment and so makes a bad choice. What brings about the sinful choice is a failure of attention.[9] Perhaps there is a failure to think about the other relevant aspects under which the object of my choice is no longer a good thing to do. (Something would satisfy a desire of mine and I fail to consider the irreparable harm my satisfaction of that desire would bring to a great many other people.) Or, perhaps there is a failure properly to apply my more general evaluative judgments to the case at hand. (I know that

9. For other discussions of failings of attention as morally culpable, see Iris Murdoch, *The Sovereignty of Good* (New York: Schocken Books, 1971); Bernard Lonergan, *Grace and Freedom* (New York: Herder and Herder, 1971); Yves Simon, *Freedom of Choice*, ed. Peter Wolff (New York: Fordham University Press, 1969).

satisfying a desire of mine at the expense of a great many other people's welfare is improper but I fail to attend to this principle when considering the case at hand.)

What accounts, however, for these forms of inattention that lead to sinful choices?

A prerequisite for such inattention is that the human intellect is not always actively knowing in either of the two ways mentioned. For the human intellect to know anything, it has to be brought to know by an inclination to consider or inquire. If the human intellect does already know something, it need not consider such knowledge at all times. The more direct causal condition for the inattention that produces a mistaken judgment is the corruptibility of human faculties: it is of the very nature of human faculties to be capable of failure, error, and mistake. The proximal occasioning causes of a failure of attention may be some source of distraction—anger, lust, irritability, physical irritants, sleepiness, and so on.

But now if human beings are brought to be by God with faculties that are inactive in this way and prone to fail (and what is prone to fail, will fail at some time or other), is not the very world God creates one of sin? One can respond that the inattention that brings about sinful choices is not itself a sin. Human beings simply do not attend to everything they know and do not always act to find out about what they do not know, and there is no sin in any of that. Should one's intellect be inactive when one is deciding on the best course of action, that is what leads to sin. There is no sin in an evaluative judgment that is mistaken because of inattention (the judgment "this is the best thing for me to do" when it is not). The sin comes in *choosing* to do that rather than directing oneself to reconsider those general principles or aspects of the situation that one could have attended to but did not. The kind of inactivity that characterizes human knowers and the corruptibility (and corruption) of human faculties can therefore be said to be a part of the world God's creative will is behind; that does not mean, however, that God is behind the sin.

It is the conjunction, then, of a failure of attention and an act of choosing that makes for a sinful choice. But what is the cause of this? Is it simply an accident that persons fail to attend properly when in the act of choosing? It is clear it is the human being who of his or her own free choice fails to attend properly in choosing; but one could say that the sinful result is accidental from the side of the human agent in that he or she does not actively intend a failure of attention to issue in a bad choice.

But is it accidental from the side of God as a creative agent? Must not God's creative will for the world include that conjunction with the knowledge that it will issue in a sinful choice? The theologian could say that failure of attention in choosing is a not-attending; it does not exist and therefore cannot be a part of what God wills as creator. But cannot God *prevent* a failure of that sort at the relevant time by making the human being's *attention* at that moment part of the world God calls forth? Our premises about creation give us no reason to deny this.

The theologian holding onto our picture can respond, however. Let us say that, even though human beings have corruptible faculties, God prevents their actual corruption. In that case human beings always properly attend when choosing what it is they want to do, although the nature of human faculties themselves gives one no reason to expect this. Does not this violate the integrity of human beings, and therefore the gracious, generous quality of God's giving that is so fundamental to our picture? Human beings are not permitted by God to be what they are—fallible beings, who tend of themselves to make mistakes.

This does not seem to me an adequate response. Why cannot God restrict the errors in judgment human beings make to those occasions when human beings are not trying to decide what to do or occasions when they simply do not choose to act on them? This would be a rather odd world but it is a possible one in which human beings would be able to demonstrate the fallibility of their own natures without sinning. If the world is not that way (and as a matter of fact it is not), God must be directly behind the conjunctions of inattention and acts of choice that make for sinful choices.

This result conflicts with the premise of God's goodness, and here I believe the theologian holding onto our picture must simply admit the limits that picture places on the intelligibility of sin. The theologian is left saying that human beings fail of their own free will to attend properly when choosing to act and this is not God's will—*whatever* the account of what specifically makes for their sinful choices, that is not God's will.

In sum, one can give an account of what sin is (a defect) that is intelligible according to our premises about God as creator. One can also give an intelligible account of what makes sinful human choices possible, say: (1) human beings are not God; (2) their faculties are not always in act and are corruptible; (3) human beings act freely (so that they sin by their own choice). But one can offer no account of how sin actually arises that does not imply that God's creative will is directly behind such an eventuality.

Can a theologian who abides by our premises give any justification for such an exception at this point? Only this I think, that what our premises about God as the creator mean is that God is the ultimate *explanation* for all that is. To say that sin is an exception to the premise of God as creator is therefore to say that sin is ultimately *without* explanation; it is what, by all rights, should not exist in a world that God creates. If a good God is the ultimate explanatory principle according to our picture, is not this inexplicable character of the coming to be of sin what one should expect?

So far we have only explored responses to the first charge mentioned above, the charge that sin conflicts with the claim of an absolute relation of dependence of all things upon God. We still need to address the other two objections mentioned, the one claiming that sin implies freedom from God, the other that, given that freedom, the infallible efficacy of God's creative working is destroyed. Let us concentrate on the last charge, that God's creative calling forth becomes fallible in a world of sin, since that charge presupposes the other, that sin involves freedom from God.

One possible strategy for maintaining God's infallibility assumes that sin can somehow exist without being called forth by God and complicates the account of God's creative intention for the world to make up for that fact. Although sin is not called forth by God, the possibility of sin's existence is *taken into account* in God's creative intention for the world, and therefore that intention remains infallible: the world happens just the way God intends it to, even should sin exist.

Here is how the argument works. God's intention for the world, the creative intention that holds up into being the whole of the world, includes sets of pseudosubjunctive propositions; propositions, that is, about what else will happen in the world should the creature sin, and what will happen within the world should the creature not. These are *pseudo*subjunctive propositions in that God knows from all eternity whether or not the creature *does* sin. Let us say God intends the salvation of all persons, then with infinite detail what God intends includes the saving of x in such and such a way y if x does not sin, and the saving of x in such and such a way z if x does sin, with the knowledge of whether or not and, if so, when, x sins. If the creature sins, that is contrary to God's will in that God's will does not extend to the bringing to be of sin. If the creature sins, what happens in the world will be different (subsequent events will be different), but *God's will* for the world will not be.

How does God know whether and when sin occurs? The only crucial point to make here (if the premises we have given above are not to be violated) is that this knowledge of the existence of sin is not a *condition* of God's forming God's very complicated intentions with respect to the world. God's knowledge of sin is dependent upon, and is logically subsequent to, God's creative intention for the world. It is therefore part of what could be called God's *practical* knowledge, or knowledge of what the created world is like in God's will for it. God does not directly will sin but sin (insofar as it is a defect) presupposes God's will for the world in which it occurs.[10]

The argument I have been making depends on multiplying, perhaps indefinitely, the outcomes that may conform to God's will for the world. But is there not a specific sort of outcome, or quite limited set of outcomes that Christians believe God wills for the world? For example, Christians claim that God wills the salvation of at least some, perhaps all, human beings. If unrepentant sinners cannot be saved, is not the possibility that all human beings are unrepentant sinners a condition upon an intention to save of that sort? In other words, God would have to know that not all human beings become unrepentant sinners *in order to form* an infallible intention to save at least some of them.

A theologian holding our picture of God as creator can respond that if God intends to save at least some people then God can assure the efficacy of that intention simply by including within it the intention to convert those people at the very moment of their deaths, should they be otherwise in an unrepentant state. If God wills that a hitherto unrepentant sinner turn himself or herself to God at the very moment of death, that conversion follows of necessity, and there are no more moments of that person's life to allow for a subsequent lapse, to allow for the renewal of that inexplicable entrance of sin. This extreme recourse of God is not of course necessary in every case; it is only necessary for those persons that God

10. This knowledge of whether or not a creature sins is therefore not by way of a so-called middle knowledge. God does not know about this sin, in other words, by knowing that *were* God to choose to create the world under certain specific initial conditions, the creature would sin in this way. If sin is freely chosen, given the same initial conditions, the creature may or may not sin, and therefore not even God can know in this way whether sin occurs. God knows that sin exists (without directly willing it) simply because it *does exist* in the world God brings about. God's omniscience means that God knows everything there is to know. God knows sin simply because sin happens.

wants to save whom God knows remain unrepentant the second before their deaths.

The bottom line here on the question of sin's interference with a claim of God's necessary efficacy is that God can prevent a lapse into sin by bringing forth at the crucial moment human choices that are not sinful. We can affirm therefore that the existence of sin cannot frustrate God's intention for the world. At most, the existence of sin brings about a different way of getting to the ends God wills, without altering God's intention about what is to happen on that supposition. With or without sin, or whatever the particular sinful choices made, the *same* end that God wants will happen. The sinners' intentions are taken up within the intention of God for the world and are inevitably redirected to the end God wills, in virtue of the fact that God's will is directly efficacious of everything else in the world besides sin and the fact that God can always will with the same necessary efficacy that a sinner's heart be transformed. The will of God for the world remains infallible, therefore, in a form much like the fate of the classical Greek tragedies—in whichever way one strikes out one will be brought back to the same point. But, now, what is fated, if one believes in the benevolence and mercy of God, is the good.

GOD THE CREATOR OF GOOD AND EVIL?

William Hasker

When I first set out to write this reply, it seemed obvious to me that Kathryn Tanner's position, in Chapter 4 and in her book,[1] is a variety of theological determinism. This still seems obvious to me, but I have learned in the meantime[2] that Tanner does not regard herself as a determinist. So it is up to me to provide some justification if I am going to refer to her view as theological determinism.

In agreement with Richard Taylor, I understand determinism to be "the general philosophical thesis which states that for everything that ever happens there are conditions such that, given them, nothing else could happen."[3] And theological determinism is determinism in which the rele-

---

1. Kathryn Tanner, *God and Creation in Christian Theology: Tyranny or Empowerment?* (Oxford: Basil Blackwell, 1988). Page citations in this chapter are to Chapter 4 in this volume.
2. Through conversations with Thomas Tracy.
3. Richard Taylor, "Determinism," in the *Encyclopedia of Philosophy*, 2:359. And compare the following definition of indeterminism from Brand Blanshard: "By indeterminism I mean

vant conditions have to do with the will and decrees of God. I think there is no doubt that, thus understood, Tanner is a theological determinist— at least until the very last pages of her essay. As she says, "A theologian holding our picture cannot deny that, given God's infallible working, human beings *must* choose when and what God wills" (page 127). (To be sure, we must not overlook Tanner's contention that only the good in the created world, and not the evil in it, derives from God. The implications of this will be considered later.)

Now it may be that Tanner has in mind some other sense of "determinism," and she may think that in this sense of the word she is not a determinist. And provided this other sense can be made tolerably clear,[4] she may well be right; it may be that she is *not* a determinist according to her own preferred meaning for that term. But this fact, if it is a fact, has no bearing whatever on the point that is at issue here, namely that she *is* a theological determinist in the sense explained in the previous paragraph. It is in this sense, and this sense only, that "theological determinism" will be used in the present discussion.

Before addressing Tanner's position, it is necessary to say something about her treatment of her opponents' views. It is unfortunately a fact that Tanner often misdescribes and distorts these views, and as a result she claims for her own position comparative advantage that does not prop-

---

the view that there is some event B that is not so connected with any previous event A that, given A, B must occur" ("The Case for Determinism," in *Determinism and Freedom in the Age of Modern Science*, ed. Sidney Hook (New York: Collier, 1958), 20.

4. This requirement is not a trivial one. To illustrate, I quote an assertion—or rather, a rhetorical question—from David Burrell's defense of Tanner's position against the criticisms of Thomas Tracy. "What," he asks, "if God's willing something to take place were not to *entail* that event's occurring?" ("Divine Action and Human Freedom in the Context of Creation," Response 3 in this volume). What indeed? If "entail" is understood in the usual way—the way in which almost any philosopher would naturally take it—then for the entailment in question not to hold would mean that it is *possible for God to will an event and yet the event not occur.* But to assert that this *is* possible would make nonsense of Tanner's and Burrell's position. I must conclude, then, that he is using "entail" in some special sense of his own, so that for A to entail B means something other than that it is impossible for A to occur and B not to occur. But since I have no idea what this new sense of "entail" might be, Burrell's rhetorical question conveys no meaning to me at all.

But (and this is the important point), even if Burrell is correct that in his special meaning of "entail" God's willing does not entail that the event occurs, it remains true that God's willing an event *does* entail the event *in the ordinary sense of "entail" that is assumed in Tracy's argument.* Providing new definitions for key terms may serve to change the subject, but has no effect whatever on the logic of the original argument.

erly belong to it. One clear example of this (among several that could be cited) is found in the following passage:

> Theologians who assume the above picture or account [i.e., Tanner's account of the relation of creator to creature] will want to say that any power or free action attributed to human beings exists in an absolute relation of dependence upon God. According to the account given above it makes no sense to claim that human beings have attributes that are good but that are not dependent upon God in that way: this would just be to say that human beings in those respects are not created. The premise that all nondivine beings exist in an absolute relation of dependence upon God would have in that case an exception. . . . [W]hat is at stake here is a proper recognition of God's beneficence. All that we have for good we have received from God. The more valuable the attribute of free agency the more the concern to claim that it is a created gift. (pages 114–15)

This is well said, but Tanner appears to think that it marks some distinctive merit of her own view. On the contrary, however, *a theological libertarian[5] can affirm everything Tanner says here*. Theological libertarians by no means hold that the powers of human beings, including the power of free choice, are self-created, nor do they think there can be anything good in human beings, their powers, and their actions, that is not the gift of God. What the theological libertarian will *not* affirm, however, is that the exercise of the gift of freedom is *controlled* by God. Tanner, it appears, is not especially enamored of this language of "control"; it is nevertheless true that this language marks *the* crucial difference between herself and her opponents.

   This distortion of her opponents' views comes close to defamation in the next paragraph, where she writes:

> Any attempt to exempt human powers from an absolute relation of dependence upon God can only be suspected, from this point

---

5. I shall use this term to designate those thinkers who affirm that human beings exert libertarian freedom *in relation to God*—the position Tanner opposes. (The qualifier "theological" is required, because Tanner maintains—erroneously, as I shall argue—that her own position is compatible with a *philosophical* libertarianism.)

of view, of Titanism. What is it that motivates the desire to exempt the greatest attributes of a specifically human existence from dependence upon God, if not the desire to be unbeholden to God in some way for the greatness of what one is? (page 115)[6]

Now, perhaps Tanner really does think that the vast majority of present-day Christians, and of Christian theologians and philosophers, are guilty of Titanism. But what are we to say when she lays such an accusation against Irenaeus, Gregory of Nyssa, Duns Scotus, William of Ockham, Luis de Molina, Francisco Suarez, Jacob Arminius, and John Wesley— not to mention the entirety of Eastern Christendom?[7] After this it is hardly a surprise when she says, a few pages later,

> If the critic insists that human choice can genuinely end with the human agent only if *God* is not also bringing about the agent choosing, is that not finally to push a theological claim? One insists that the nonnecessitated character of human choice be taken so far that *human beings are no longer creatures*. (page 126, second emphasis added)

So theological libertarians not only are guilty of Titanism; they go so far as to deny that they are created by God!

To be sure, the breezy insouciance with which all this is said takes some of the sting out of it. But it simply is not acceptable to take a central Christian doctrine like that of creation, give it your own somewhat idiosyncratic meaning, and then when fellow Christians do not agree, to charge them with denying the doctrine in question.[8] And there is another reason why Tanner should not be too harsh in her judgment of theological

6. It's true that Tanner says that "[t]he theologian inclined to exempt human agency from the sort of relation of dependence upon God I've specified will have, of course, his or her *own* reasons for doing so," and she goes on to speculate about what those reasons might be. But this changes nothing. Either Tanner accepts that those other reasons really *are* the reasons for the position in question, or she does not. If she does accept this, then the accusation of Titanism is pointless and should be withdrawn. If, on the other hand, she does not accept it, then the situation stands exactly as stated in the text.

7. Tanner might be inclined to deny that these theologians are in fact theological libertarians. If so, I believe she is mistaken, but it is obvious the point cannot be argued here.

8. Note that Tanner does *not* say that the *free actions* of human beings are not created by God—a claim that theological libertarians might well endorse. What she says is, that in the libertarian view the *human beings themselves* are not creatures of God.

libertarians—a reason that will become apparent in the course of the present discussion.

Turning to more substantive matters, what are we to make of Tanner's claim that her theological determinism is consistent with a philosophical libertarian view of free will? She is quite correct in asserting—and she makes this point at some length—that a theological determinist need not assert that human actions are determined *at the creaturely level;* she need not assent to logical fatalism, or physical determinism, or even to psychological determination by "the strongest motive." But is it correct to call such a combination of views libertarianism? I do not think so, for at least two reasons. First of all, it is simply a fact that libertarianism has always been defined as a view *in opposition to* all forms of determinism, not as a view of free will that is *consistent with* determinism. But Tanner clearly *is* a determinist; therefore she cannot be a libertarian.

A second reason goes somewhat deeper. The natural way to describe a libertarian view of free will is in terms of the "two-way power" attributed to the free agent: the agent has the power to perform the action in question, and also has the power to refrain from performing such an action.[9] But, further, it is necessary that the power in question be one that could actually be exercised *given all the circumstances as they exist at the time of the action;* "powers" that, for some reason or other, *cannot* be exercised in the specific situation are not the kinds of powers required for libertarian free will. Because of this, definitions of libertarianism standardly refer to the circumstances of the action, in order to stipulate that there is nothing in the circumstances that prevents the agent *either* from performing the action *or* from refraining from it. For example, consider the following definition of libertarian free will by Thomas Flint: "An agent is truly free with respect to an action only if the situation in which he is placed is logically and causally compatible with both his performing and his not performing the action."[10]

The importance of this point lies in the fact that this definition clearly *excludes* the existence of an efficacious divine decree that determines what the agent shall do in the situation. It is not the case, as Tanner supposes, that one first sets out a libertarian conception of free will and

---

9. Such claims, to be sure, leave one open to the dreaded "Frankfurt counterexamples." There is no space to discuss these counterexamples here, but I believe they are greatly overrated.

10. Thomas P. Flint, "The Problem of Divine Freedom," *American Philosophical Quarterly* 20 (1983): 255.

then must decide whether or not to *add* to that conception the stipulation that God has not predetermined the agent's choice. Rather, the basic definition of free will *already* excludes such divine determination; so that in order to get a "libertarianism" consistent with theological determinism one would have to *qualify* the definition of free will so as to specify that only the *creaturely* situation need be "compatible with both his performing and not performing the action," while leaving it open that when *God* is considered only one of the two choices may really be possible. But I do not know of any libertarians who would accept this kind of restriction on the definition of free will, so I judge that Tanner's view is not properly termed "libertarian."

However the terminological issue is to be resolved, Tanner clearly thinks her theological determinism should be more acceptable than determination by natural causes. But it is not at all clear that this is so. If I were to discover that some action of mine, which I thought was freely chosen, was in fact the result of some random combination of physical circumstances, I should probably be somewhat upset. But I should be a great deal *more* upset were I to discover that my "free" action was the result of the deliberate control of me by *some other person*, someone who caused me so to act while leaving me unaware of that fact. Nor is it clear to me (though here Tanner would certainly disagree) that things are a great deal better if it is God rather than another human being who is doing the controlling. But the most serious objections to theological determinism stem from the facts of moral evil, facts that constitute Tanner's principal topic in the present essay, even though they occupy relatively few of its pages.

These pages are devoted by Tanner to answering two objections, of which the first is that "[s]inful choices present an exception to our premises about creation," in that "[s]ome aspect of nondivine being exists without being in an absolute relation of dependence upon God's will for it" (page 129). Her response, briefly summarized, is as follows: sin is not an existing being, but a lack, a defect; nevertheless, as parasitic on God's good creation it remains absolutely dependent on God. This defect is, furthermore, not the result of a positive *action* on the creature's part but rather of an *inaction*—a failure, for example, to consider the respect in which the object of some choice of mine is not a good thing to do, or a failure to apply my general evaluative principles to the present case. So "[i]t is the conjunction . . . of a failure of attention and an act of choosing that makes for a sinful choice" (page 131).

Now, one could very well question whether this description applies to *all* cases of sinful choice that actually occur. But leaving that aside, we are still left with a question: Why doesn't God prevent failure of attention on those occasions when it would lead to sinful choices? Unwilling to say that God is "directly behind the conjunctions of inattention and acts of choice that make for sinful choices," Tanner is forced to admit that "sin is an exception to the premise of God as creator" and "is ultimately *without* explanation." She goes on to argue that the inexplicability of sin is to be expected and is thus not a defect of her account: "If a good God is the ultimate explanatory principle according to our picture, isn't this inexplicable character of the coming to be of sin what one should expect?" (page 133).

But neither God nor Tanner can be let off this easily. Consider a specific case, in which (for example) a man is deciding whether or not to tell the truth about a disreputable incident in his past. If he attends to the ethical requirement of truth-telling and applies it to the present case, he will tell the truth; otherwise he will lie about the incident. Now, suppose he does indeed tell the truth. Is it possible that he should do so, absent God's efficacious decree to that effect? On Tanner's general account, the answer would seem to be no, it is *not* possible that he should tell the truth unless God so decrees. But if that is so, then God's so decreeing is a *necessary condition* of his telling the truth. But then it follows that God's failure to decree that he should tell the truth is a *sufficient condition* of his choosing to lie, and we have once again the result that God is "directly behind the conjunctions of inattention and acts of choice that make for sinful choices," a conclusion which, by Tanner's own admission, "conflicts with the premise of God's goodness" (page 132).[11]

There would be a way around this, to be sure, if we were to hold that God decrees *neither* that the agent shall attend to the requirement of truth-telling *nor* that he shall fail to so attend. On this assumption, what God decrees is that the agent shall be confronted with such a choice, but God makes no decree whatever about *how* the choice shall be made. This

---

11. The claim that the divine decree is the cause of good actions but not of sinful actions may remind some readers of the controversy over single versus double predestination. In both cases, the claim that only the "good" result is decreed tends to soften the resulting picture of God, but at the cost of a certain loss of logical coherence. As Richard Swinburne says, "If all and only those who are saved are programmed in advance to be saved, then those who are lost will be so as a result of not being programmed, i.e. they will have been reprobated" (*Responsibility and Atonement* [Oxford: Clarendon Press, 1989], 193).

would indeed enable Tanner to avoid the direct connection between sin and God's will, but it seems to be inconsistent with everything she has said up to this point. Nevertheless, a consideration of her answer to the second objection may lead us to wonder whether this is after all what she has in mind.

The second objection is that, given the freedom with respect to God implied by sin, "the infallible efficacy of God's creative working is destroyed," so that "God's creative calling forth becomes fallible in a world of sin." Her response is that "[a]lthough sin is not called forth by God, the possibility of sin's existence is *taken into account* in God's creative intention for the world" (page 133). In spelling this out, she writes:

> God's intention for the world, the creative intention that holds up into being the whole of the world, includes sets of pseudosubjunctive propositions. Propositions, that is, about what else will happen in the world should the creature sin, and what will happen within the world should the creature not. These are *pseudo*-subjunctive propositions in that God knows from all eternity whether or not the creature *does* sin. Let us say God intends the salvation of all persons, then with infinite detail what God intends includes the saving of x in such and such a way y if x does not sin, and the saving of x in such and such a way z if x does sin, with the knowledge of whether or not and, if so, when, x sins. If the creature sins, that is contrary to God's will in that God's will does not extend to the bringing to be of sin. If the creature sins, what happens in the world will be different (subsequent events will be different), but *God's will* for the world will not be. (page 133)

Note first of all that there is no need to refer to the propositions in question as *pseudo*subjunctives, since ordinary subjunctive propositions do *not* entail or logically presuppose that the one who asserts them is ignorant of the truth-value of the antecedent. These propositions are subjunctives, period; there is nothing "pseudo" about them. In responding to the question, "How does God know whether and when sin occurs?" Tanner stresses that God's "knowledge of the existence of sin is not a *condition* of God's forming of God's very complicated intentions with respect to the world. God's knowledge of sin is dependent upon, and is logically consequent to, God's creative intention for the world" (page

134). So God first forms his intentions for the world, expressed in sub-junctive propositions; subsequent to this it turns out that, on a given occasion, the human agent either sins or refrains from sinning, and God's *will* is executed in a different way depending on which of these is the case.

Tanner admits that her argument "depends on multiplying, perhaps indefinitely, the outcomes that may conform to God's will for the world" (page 134). In other words, there are *many* ways God's will can be ful-filled, *depending on the decisions of the human agents.* She goes on to consider whether God's will may in the process become fallible, in that (for example) if all sinners were to remain unrepentant God would be unable to save anyone.

Now that is a good question, and of course Tanner is not the first to raise it. It is often, for instance, raised against "free-will theists" by their Molinist opponents.[12] What may seem remarkable, however, is that such a question should arise within the context of a deterministic position like Tanner's. But in view of these latest moves, is Tanner still a determinist? Hasn't she in effect abandoned her insistence that "human beings *must* choose when and what God wills"? In leaving it up to the *human agent* whether the agent sins or refrains from sinning, hasn't she crossed the Rubicon and become a theological libertarian?

There is, to be sure, one way in which she could avoid this. She could adopt the view suggested earlier, according to which God, by his effica-cious decree, determines the occurrence of any virtuous or nonsinful response to an occasion of temptation. If on the other hand God does *not* decree a nonsinful response, a necessary condition for such a response is lacking and so the agent, inevitably though without a specific divine decree, yields to the temptation and commits sin. But it seems to be clearly her view (and rightly so, in my estimation) that this "conflicts with the premise of God's goodness" and cannot be accepted. If this were indeed her view, there would be no need whatever to multiply "the out-comes that may conform to God's will for the world," as we have just seen that she does. But if she does not take this way out, then it is as was said above: whether sin occurs or not depends on the human agent and not upon God.

And now we are able to see why it is that Kathryn Tanner would be

---

12. For my own discussion of the question, see "Providence and Evil: Three Theories," *Religious Studies* 28 (1992): 103–4.

well advised to moderate her judgments on theological libertarians. She ought to speak gently to us because, under the pressure of the problem of moral evil, she has become one of us herself. For my part, I am happy to congratulate her on her theological good sense and to welcome her into the fold.

INDEX

action, divine
    direct, 44–45, 84–87, 91–96, 100, 113–14
    indirect, 88–92, 100
    particular, or special, 4–7, 22–25, 37, 39, 41–46, 59–62, 83, 100
    noninterventionist account of, 23–29, 36, 39–40, 57–61
    See also double agency; God as creator; grace, divine; miracle
actions, basic, 45, 81–82, 94, 98
Adams, Marilyn, 85 n. 11
Alston, William, 81 n. 7, 89 n. 14
Aquinas, Thomas, 66, 95 n. 19, 104, 106–9
Augustine, 99

Barth, Karl, 16, 66, 73, 112
Bible, 1–3, 18–21, 64–66
Bonhoeffer, Dietrich, 66
Bultmann, Rudolph, 77–78
Burrell, David, 138 n. 4

Calvin, John, 67
causation, 85, 117–20
chance, 91
Christ, 69
    resurrection of, 28, 36
    virginal conception of, 27
Cicero, 68–69

determinism, 38–39, 46–49, 89–90, 92, 137–38
double agency, 7, 79–80, 97–99, 101, 103–4

ethics, theological, 71–74
evil, problem of, 3, 5–6, 9, 55–56, 70
    free-will reply to, 5, 16, 22, 33–35, 38–39
experience of God, 60–61, 67–68

Farrer, Austin, 7, 79–83, 105
Flew, Antony, 4 n. 3
Flint, Thomas, 141
foreknowledge, divine, 43–44, 93 n. 18, 134–35
freedom, 7–9, 54–55, 92–97, 99–101, 108, 111, 114–17, 121–29, 139, 141–42, 145. *See also* evil, problem of, free-will reply
Fuller, Reginald, 3 n. 1

Gilkey, Langdon, 3 n. 1, 46–47
Gimaret, Daniel, 107 n. 4
God
    as creator, 7–9, 25, 58–59, 62, 83–85, 89–90, 104–6, 112–14
    as impersonal power, 6, 64–71
    infallible will of, 94–96, 120, 125–28, 133–35, 144–45
    as personal agent, 6, 52–54
    personal relationship with, 37–40
    and time, 42, 44 n. 4
    See also action, divine; foreknowledge, divine
grace, 54, 80, 97, 98 n. 22
Gutierrez, Gustavo, 65